D1447196

NEWS FROM SOMEWHERE

News From Somewhere
On Settling

ROGER SCRUTON

continuum
LONDON • NEW YORK

Continuum
The Tower Building, 11 York Road, London SE1 7NX
15 East 26th Street, New York, NY 10010

All rights reserved. No part of this publication may be reproduced or
transmitted in any form or by any means, electronic or mechanical,
including photocopying, recording or any information storage or
retrieval system, without prior permission in writing from the publishers.

First published 2004

Copyright © Roger Scruton 2004

British Library Cataloguing in Publication Data
A catalogue record for this book is available from the British Library.

ISBN 0-8264-6930-2

Typeset in Postscript Sabon by Tony Lansbury, Tonbridge, Kent.

Printed by CPI Group (UK) Ltd, Croydon CR0 4YY

1

MIX
Paper from
responsible sources
FSC   FSC® C013604
www.fsc.org

Contents

Preface

West of Swindon, North of the Vale of White Horse and adjoining the Southern slopes of the Cotswolds, lie the Wiltshire claylands – low hills and plateaux that were once partly covered by the Royal forest of Braydon. The Kimmeridge clay runs to a depth of 500 feet under Swindon; Malmesbury sits on Oxford clay, which is in places only 10 feet thick. Whatever the thickness, however, clay subsoil produces a particular kind of landscape, and a particular kind of agriculture. The topsoil is supported by an impermeable underlay, which retains moisture through the summer. The fertile layer is usually too thin to admit ploughing, and the grass too lush to merit the attempt at it. Hence the claylands remain today what they have been since the Forest of Braydon was first cleared in the late Middle Ages: pasture meadows, supporting cattle and sheep, divided by hedgerows of quickthorn, sycamore, elder, willow and ash. Thirty years ago the hedges were punctuated by elms, which from a distance gave the appearance of a majestic light-filled forest. Broader, fuller, but less tall, stood ash and oak, some surviving from the Forest of Braydon, others self-seeded in the centuries since.

The elms died, but the landscape of the claylands has retained its wooded appearance, with oak-trees standing in the hedgerows, hillocks crowned by ash and maple, and long strings of spinneys in the vale. Water is retained at every height, and even in the driest summer you will find dew-ponds on the hill-tops, and marshy hollows on the slopes. Some of the ponds support moor-hens, rails, mallards and grebes, and often you can see, standing motionless in the shallows, the battleship-grey of a heron, eyeing the dark water for silver fish and tench.

The claylands are home to small family farms, some of them no bigger than 50 acres, and most of them dependent on dairy cows, beef cattle and sheep. Small farms mean frequent boundaries; hedgerows in the claylands have therefore been continuously maintained, even during the post-war years when the Government subsidized their destruction. During those same years Wiltshire County Council, in an effort to arrest the depopulation of the countryside, built small farms of its own, to be rented out to those de-mobilized soldiers who had conceived rustic yearnings during their time in uniform. Among the old farmsteads of timber and Cotswold stone, therefore, you will come across boxes of council-house brick, with metal-framed windows and concrete outbuildings reminiscent of the camps and barracks that littered our countryside after the war. The growth of light industry in Swindon has meant an influx of commuters to the villages, which have bubbled out in estates of 'executive homes'. But the farmland itself remains as it has been for centuries: cow-speckled pastures in summer, grazed off by sheep in the autumn, and left to recuperate through the winter months, when the rain washes out the divots and the bare patches come alive again as grass.

North of the village of Brinkworth, bounded to the west by the ancient borough of Malmesbury, to the north by the Malmesbury-Cricklade road, and to the east by Webb's Wood and Somerford Common – two surviving fragments of the Forest of Braydon – lies a string of small hills, where the old economy of the claylands endures, altered by the demands of modern life, but rooted, for all that, in customs that are part of the landscape. Narrow roads wind between farms that bear names familiar since records began: Braydonside, Washpool, Stoppers Hill, Moor Lane, Pink Lane, Rouslands, Sundey Hill.[1] Once the property of the Abbot of Malmesbury, to whom they had been given by Leofsige, a Saxon nobleman, then granted at the Dissolution to William Stumpe, a wealthy clothier who bought the entire Abbey Estate, these farms were subsequently inherited by the Earls of Suffolk who retained them until the 1960s, when death duties forced their sale. They are places of deep settlement, where families draw their nourishment as trees draw nourishment from the soil. And the farmers bear their increasing burdens as trees bear the weather, knowing that to be uprooted is to die.

You see this tenacity by day, in the resourceful industry whereby the farmers turn each misfortune to some small advantage, improvising their way through debt, disease and regulation to the point where they can replace their stock and plan for another year. And you see it by night, when darkness descends over this sequestered landscape and all at once you are aware of its disconnection from the surrounding world of entropy and waste. To one side is the orange glow of Swindon, invading the night and extinguishing the stars; across the Vale of the White Horse are the bright flares of Lyneham airbase, raised high on gantries, and burning away the darkness for miles around. Further still is a row of street lights, like cold staring eyes, placed on the far horizon by a local council with money to spare. In this coralled landscape, however, the Great Bear still swings slowly around the pole, and the Milky Way lies like a silken scarf from horizon to horizon. This is the only pocket between Swindon and Bristol where you encounter that most precious commodity, and the one that attaches you to the countryside more than any other, which is the night.

If farmers go out at night they take a torch, and they are aware that its beam stirs up the hedgerows as a stick stirs up a pond. They understand that it is a violence against the animals, to deprive them of the darkness. Domestic animals too are happier without electric light, adjusting their body rhythms unerringly to the short days of winter and the short summer nights. And the farmer who looks after animals rises with the dawn and becomes dormant at dusk as they do. One light in the kitchen is all that he needs, and for the most part it is all that you see when you look across the fields at night towards the farmsteads. The punctuated darkness of the claylands is proof that the land has not been erased by the people who live in it, but that land and people take their character from each other. That is what we mean or ought to mean by countryside, and it is why the suburbs are a world apart from it.

In *News from Nowhere* William Morris described his socialist utopia: a version of the English countryside, purged of real people, inoculated against religion, and sprinkled all over with a kind of medieval star-dust. The nowhere of William Morris has since stepped down from the realm of utopian fantasy to become the nowhere of the American exurbia – the placeless, faceless wasteland described and deplored by James Howard Kunstler.[2] Morris's fantasy was possible only because he had a real somewhere of his own: Kelmscott, where he was living and working while composing his preposterous book. And it was while hunting at Kelmscott that I decided to follow Morris's example: to settle not nowhere, but somewhere within the boundaries of the Vale of the White Horse hunt. Hunting was the activity that drew me, as it drew John Jorrocks, Surtees' cockney shopkeeper, away from the city and back to the land. Because of hunting I had become self-employed, had rented a cottage, and was looking for the place that would be mine. And it was a hunting farmer from the claylands who told me of the run-down thirty-acre sheep farm near to his that was about to come on the market.

It was thus that, 10 years ago, I came to Sunday Hill Farm, bringing with me a library, three pianos and four horses. I was the first 'off-comer' to attempt to settle among families that had farmed here for centuries. Eight of the nearest farms were owned by people with only three surnames between them, and these surnames – Lewis, Scott and Webb – are to be found throughout the claylands, borne by farmers and their spouses, and also by fields, farms and woodlands.

Sunday Hill Farm is an old cottage of Cotswold stone, with a stone barn attached to one side of it. My first act on moving in was to replace the metal-framed windows and to cover the grim concrete extension with a veneer of rendering. So far as I could see nobody in the valley had ever before carried out building work for aesthetic reasons. It was a dangerous thing to do; still more dangerous to pull down three sheds built from panels of some hideous aggregate with an appearance of dried vomit. I was acutely aware of the eyes observing me, of the suppressed indignation at the sight of useful things destroyed, and of the insult to farming implied by my bourgeois need for things to look right, rather than to work right. For my neighbours the landscape was reality – the source of their livelihood, and the recipient of their toil. For me it was appearance – the view from my window, my 'sweet especial rural scene'. My presence in this rustic redoubt was bound to be seen as a danger: I was announcing the imminent triumph of town over country, of the romantic love of appearance over the healthy use of things. I was there to etherealize my neighbours, and to write their epitaph. So it must have seemed to them at least, and during my first months, as I struggled to put down roots in soil that does not take kindly to imported varieties, the vagueness with which my plans were endorsed and my greetings accepted left me in no doubt that my neighbours looked on the prospect of a farm without a farmer as a premonition and a threat.

Settling is not something you do on your own. It is a social event, an act of corporate inclusion, in which the landscape receives you through the gestures of its long-term inhabitants. If everyone were as mobile, geographically, socially and culturally, as I had been, then settling would be impossible. I was aware of this, and also ashamed of it. My neighbours had something that I was seeking, and I had nothing to give in return.

However, it is a truth universally acknowledged, that a single man in possession of a house and 30 acres must be in want of a wife. And it was in those first anxious months as a landowner that I discovered her. I fell in love with a girl whom I had seen poised aloft in the Beaufort colours, a free but disciplined, lively but discarnate being, presented by the hunting uniform like a painted angel in a frame. When, after many hesitations, I invited her to dinner and she arrived in ordinary clothes it was as though she had stepped down from the picture, bringing with her the charm, the courtesy and the other-wordly order that prevailed within it. Since that time I can never see Sophie in her Beaufort uniform without a thrill of recognition, as though revisiting a dream.

My attempt to settle has had an added charm for me, therefore, in being conducted in tandem with an old-fashioned courtship – one that progressed slowly but without trouble towards marriage and children. In what follows I describe the rural world not as I discovered it, but as we discovered it together. We explored our little patch like birds, bringing home the odds and ends of information, machinery, friendship, furniture and gossip which, woven together, now form the nest that is our home.

Much of the material in this book has appeared in articles written in the course of my work as a freelance journalist, and I am indebted to the editors of the *Financial Times*, *openDemocracy. net*, *Hunting Magazine*, *The Spectator*, *The Times*, the *Sunday Telegraph*, the *New Statesman* and the *Daily Mail*. In putting the book together I have changed names and transposed details in the interests of privacy. But what follows is a true record of an existing form of life – one in which the land itself is the central character.

Malmesbury, Christmas 2003

1

Our Soil

Pieter Brueghel's painting of the fall of Icarus shows one helpless leg of the presumptious aeronaut as he disappears beneath the waves. The rest of the world – the galleon tacking into port, the peasant driving a plough, the solitary angler, the shepherd with his dog – all these seem unaffected by the strange event. Only the shepherd has noticed it, raising his eyes to a point in the sky long since vacated by the falling Icarus. It is as if Brueghel is deliberately negating the description of the scene that he found in Ovid, who also includes a fisherman 'angling for fish with his flexible rod ... a shepherd, leaning upon his crook ... a ploughman gripping his plough-handles', but who describes them as standing stupefied, watching what they take to be the flight of gods.[3] For Brueghel mortal life proceeds as if these bold experiments, leading to both triumph and disaster, have so little significance as to be barely perceivable. Hence many people see the point of this painting as Auden did:

> *how everything turns away*
> *Quite leisurely from the disaster; the ploughman may*
> *Have heard the splash, the forsaken cry,*
> *But for him it was not an important failure ...*[4]

Look more closely, however, and another meaning emerges. The geometrical and chromatic harmony of Brueghel's composition leads the eye to accept what is in fact an endless array of spatial dissonances. The galleon, seen in relation to the shore, is miniscule, like a toy, and Icarus's leg beside it as large as a whale. Both are close by the shore from one perspective, and half-a-mile out to sea from another. The shepherd seems to stand hundreds of feet above the water: trace the land beneath him to the shore, however, and you will descend only a yard or two. The ploughman, appearing 50 or more feet above the shepherd, is tilling a field that seems to terminate in a cliff just a few yards higher than the field where the shepherd stands. The furrow goes, impossibly, to the very edge of the cliff, and the horse is plodding onwards indifferent to the danger. In the distance a city stands at the water's edge, the buildings unnaturally large in perspective, but also unnaturally small beside the boats that are plying its harbour. No episode in this picture belongs with any other, and the apparent harmony is an illusion, engineered by the painter's mastery of line and colour, but no more real than the space in an Escher woodcut.

Spatial dissonance is matched by temporal dissonance. The sun lies on the horizon. It must therefore be sunset, if the sun is to have melted Icarus's wings. Yet the light is the yellow light of dawn, and the shadows are faint and powdery like shadows in the middle of the day. Moreover the melting of the wax must have occurred when the sun was overhead, and Icarus too bold in his approach to it. Dawn, midday and sunset compete for our belief in them, and all are unbelievable.

A single figure demands our attention, and that is the ploughman. His vermilion shirt is the one place of concentrated colour, his bent form the one source of focused energy, and his downturned inscrutable face the one object of fully realized sympathy, in a painting where everything else seems accidental, scattered and remote from us. The soil that he ploughs is virgin soil, and it turns compliantly like butter; one of his feet has landed on earth already ploughed, the other pushes off from the grass. His little plot of earth is at the very edge of things, squeezed between the mountains and the sea. But it is a plot without edges, at once intensely local and unhedged against the wider world. That world contains trade, adventure, experiment; it is a place where people sail and also fly, tempting the gods. It is a place of mislocated and dislocated people. Yet the ploughman does not see it. His thoughts and his actions focus on one thing only – the place where he is settled and which, by ploughing, he makes his own. The view from his cliff, so exciting to the wanderer, is a view that he has never observed. Through settling he has turned a plot of earth to his purposes, become one with it, and also ceased to notice where it is.

Hence settling is precarious. The edges of our land are indeterminate and dangerous; the furrow ends in nothingness; this settled place is like every other place in the picture: both somewhere and nowhere. Nowhere becomes somewhere when we settle there; but in doing so we court another kind of danger. Brueghel reminds us that this connection to the soil that keeps our eyes turned downwards removes us from the surrounding world. Rootedness is a source of strength and virtue; but the rooted person is the last to adapt to unforeseeable change. In any great transition it is the peasants who are dispossessed. And when they are not dispossessed by force, like the victims of Lenin, Stalin and Mao, they are dispossessed by the invisible hand of enterprise, like the people I describe in this book:

> But times are alter'd; trade's unfeeling train
> Usurp the land and dispossess the swain.

Goldsmith's lines, written two-and-a-half centuries ago, suggest that even if times are altered, the plight of farmers remains the same.

In all of us is still implanted the desire for the soil and for a life attached to it. Soil-worship is not confined to English writers and artists. It has inspired settlers and wanderers in America: the Southern Agrarians, for instance, whose poet laureate, Allen Tate, wrote some of the most beautiful evocations of Dixieland and the people who were rooted there; and there again the Beats, who hit the road like Jack Kerouac in search of the authentic characters who would never dream of doing any such thing. It has inspired the settlers and wanderers of France – Jean Giono and Gustave Thibon among the first, Zola and Valéry among the second. It has inspired those who have settled in foreign lands, like Patrick Leigh Fermor and John Berger, and those like Richard Jefferies who wandered around their childhood home (in Jefferies' case, a home adjacent to mine). It has produced some of the greatest literature of modern times – from *Anna Karenina* to *Four Quartets*. And it has been the dominant theme of English art and music throughout the twentieth century.

But, seen this way as an object of worship and a source of moral strength, the soil has an abstract, quasi-theological character. It sinks from view behind its representations, rather as the gods vanish behind their statues or the saints behind the icons through which they are adored. Its status as a 'primal element' is itself a kind of theological construct: for after all, we know very well that the theory of the elements was a first shot at science and one that fell hopelessly wide, so that if we still adhere to it this is only because it is no longer science for us but faith or poetry. The soil, as projected heavenwards by Lawrence, Massingham, Thibon and Giono, and whose image is caressed with such tenderness by their words, has little or no relation to the stiff, sticky, obstinate muck against which the farmer finds himself pitted.

It is a cliché to describe farmers as rooted in the soil. Clichés would not be clichés if they did not contain a core of truth; but they lead us to the truth too easily, and so prevent us from feeling it. Martin Amis tells us at all costs to avoid clichés; I think rather that we should rescue them. Maybe the redemption of the cliché is the great task for modern literature. But, after Zola, Lawrence and Faulkner, how can we rejuvenate this tired old story of the soul and the soil? Consider this, from the celebrated first chapter of Lawrence's *The Rainbow*:

> *Their life and inter-relations were such: feeling the pulse and body of the soil, that opened to the furrow for the grain and became smooth and supple after their ploughing, and clung to their feet with a weight that pulled like desire…*

Like *desire*? For our neighbours the soil pulls like a hangman at the heels of his victim. Or consider this, in a passage from one of America's New Agrarians:

> *The soil is the great connector of lives, the source and destination of all. It is the healer and restorer and resurrector, by which disease is passed into health, age into youth, death into life. Without proper care for it we have no community, because without proper care for it we have no life. It is alive itself. It is a grave, too, of course.*

The writer is Wendell Berry, currently enjoying an upsurge of popularity as the movement for organic farming takes wing in his homeland. But only in the last sentence of that encomium do we stub our toe against a truth. For our neighbours in the claylands the soil is neither a healer, nor a restorer nor a resurrector, but the cause of arthritis and back strain in themselves, of mud fever, udder rash, worms and foot-rot in their animals. Our curmudgeonly soil turns health into sickness, youth into age; and life, in due course, into death.

Sophie and I were pondering Berry's clichés on a day when, after the relentless buffeting of winter rains, the sun revisited our fields. There is a saying in our neighbourhood that the difference between a good farmer and a bad farmer is exactly one day: the critical day between winter and summer when the soil is not so wet that the machines will stick in it, and not so dry that it won't budge beneath its crust. This saying is not universally true; but it is surely true of those condemned to clay. How unfriendly, how contemptuous of human need and comfort is this soil that passes from mud to brick and back again, with scarcely a day of benevolence between! It is like some nagging companion, who changes tactics only to find some new way of frustrating you. It is not surprising if so many of our neighbours are sour, being yoked for life to an enemy, and depending on that enemy for life. John Aubrey noticed it, over three centuries ago:

> *In North Wiltshire, and like the vale of Gloucester (a dirty clayey country) the Indiginae, or Aborigines … are phlegmatique, skins pale and livid, slow and dull, heavy of spirit … melancholy, contemplative and malicious.*[5]

Something of that remains true today. We thought of the farmers among whom Sophie was brought up, of the same stock as our neighbours and with the same bundle of surnames, but settled 15 miles away, on the clean, drained, chalky soil below the Cotswolds. It came home to us how our trips to her village are holidays. Faces there are less troubled, manners more open, conversation more free. And we too, we recognized, were becoming obstinate and curmudgeonly, having to deal day after day with this primordial glue where nothing grows save grass, and the weeds like buttercup and thistle that even grass cannot stifle. Supposing a farm came up for sale in that nearby Eden, shouldn't we try to move there?

And then we remembered the saying about the good farmer and the bad. We remembered that the logs from the laid hedge must be collected, that the fields must be rolled, that the docks must be sprayed and the fences repaired. This was the day when the fight begins – the one day in the year when the fields can be forced to pay what they owe us.

Within a few hours the tractor was stuck in one place, the roller in another, the Land Rover in a third. We had scored a hay-field with ruts, left brontosaurus footprints on the cow-pasture, abandoned a trailer of logs on the hillside, and heard the mirthless laughter from the clay beneath our feet. It was the worst possible moment for Stephen to arrive – Stephen, who has farmed here all his life, who shares our hay crop, and who depends on our fields for his livelihood. Stephen's world is one of doings, not sayings. A cloud of silence moves with him around the farmyard, and his small fierce gestures are like strategic defences, constantly shooting down the encroaching dialogue. But the sight of our blunders stung him into speech, and he cursed our foolish efforts to be useful; beneath them, he implied, lay a malign desire to be worse than useless. One by one Stephen itemized our failings, and all his accumulated anger against the clay poured out of him, directed not to the soil which had shaped him, but to these ignorant incomers who had unshaped the soil. He was defending, with every breath in his outraged body, the enemy whose destiny was bound up with his.

I meekly conceded. What most afflicted me was the fact that each paragraph was rounded with an invoice. Stephen would have to roll the fields, but he would have to charge for it; each breakage from these ruts would be accounted for, each broken tine of the harrow and each blunted blade of the mower would be a debit. And with every addition to the bill there came the same sigh of bitterness, that the sums in which this soil could deal were so ungenerous: a tenner here, a fiver there, sometimes just a pound or two. 'If you had to live from farming,' Stephen concluded, 'you'd take some care; but no, you're the lucky ones.'

I wanted to say that I do live from farming – from writing about it. And Stephen survives because of the subsidy brought by my second-order farming. I am a metafarmer. And that means, I would have gone on to say, had we both belonged to the frivolous world of the university, that we are both of us farming, only my farming is meta than yours.

Then I reflected on the truth concealed within that cliché about the soil: if no farming took place here, our metafarming would cease; but the reverse could never happen. Whatever we did, Stephen must go on farming; like his father, and his father's father before him, he is locked in combat with this grudging subsoil and nothing can ever release him. His hopes and fears are centred forever on that day between summer and winter, when he will either win the year or lose it. And that was the day we had spoiled.

The enmity of the soil shows itself in another way in winter. In October you become aware, almost overnight, of the distinction between dry soil and wet. Dry soil is self-contained, discreet and reticent. While it lasts it seems the very epitome of dependableness. Wet soil is belligerent, invasive, coating everything with a veneer of slime. It maintains a running commentary on rural life, in which certainties are put in question and solid things dissolved.

Hence our neighbours dislike no time of year as much as the moment in October when the fields refuse to absorb more rain, and the cows begin to churn up the pasture. It is the moment when the animals take their revenge, remaking the landscape as a warm bath, friendly to four-legged creatures, hostile to man. The faces of the horses, as they watch you slither towards them, express their sudden bliss: 'four legs good, two legs bad', and a laugh of triumph sounds somewhere under the hillside.

Not for long, however. When wet and warm, the land is heaven to the herds. When wet and cold it is hell. In mid October their attitude suddenly changes, and there they are each morning at the gate, begging to come in from the cold. This is the moment when the bond between farmer and herd is finally sealed – when the reality of the farm, as a homestead, a shelter, a place of cohabitation and concord, is finally acknowledged by both sides to the contract. There is something ineffably soothing about the quiet stable of horses, the barn filled with the gentle shuffling of cows, the elements shut out and the farmer finally accepted by the animals as the benign and necessary minister to their small requirements. Especially at night is the renewed harmony felt, as these creatures, which do not sleep but merely lapse into a contented silence, quietly breathe in the darkness. It could be that this experience of oneness with protected animals is the true reason why people stay farming. It is an experience that brings with it a deep sense of locality. The farmer is not merely living in a particular place, but *dwelling* there, sovereign over the herd, and belonging where they belong, who belong to him. That is why, when a livestock farmer can no longer make ends meet, he does not sell up and join the dole queue in the city. He nods goodbye to his herd, then turns away and shoots himself.

This also explains the attitude of the farmer to the soil. In the Wiltshire claylands farmers do everything they can to keep the soil at bay. They cover it with scalpings, concrete it over, or ram it full of hardcore. As soon as the winter comes, they turn their backs on the fields to struggle with the more manageable mud of the farmyard. Rain on concrete is a cleansing force, the sole natural ally in the war against the soil; rain on the fields is an adjunct of the enemy.

This explains, too, why the aesthetic sense of the farmer is so different from that of the urban incomer. The incomer sees his old stone cottage as part of the landscape, which must blend in and harmonize. The farmer sees his farmstead as a refuge from the landscape, a place apart, where he and his animals can finally shake off the soil. Steel-clad barns with asbestos roofs surrounded by concrete yards symbolize his triumph over the natural order, and his ability to keep a herd of cattle alive in the teeth of the elements. Paradoxically, the very fact that his farm is such an eyesore, that it does not 'fit in', may be, for him, a proof of its fittingness, and of the fact that he does not live here because he chooses, but dwells here because he must.

In art and literature the plough is a symbol of settlement, as it is in Brueghel's painting. The 'flaxen-headed ploughboy' of the English folksong is the icon of innocent simplicity – and he jettisons both innocence and simplicity as he rises up the social scale and becomes a townie. But the plough has a peculiar status in the culture of the claylands. One of our fields is called 'Plough Piece', though it has not been tilled in living memory. When people round here use the plough, it is only to re-seed their pastures – usually with Italian rye-grass, which in a good year will give two or even three cuts of silage. Over the hill, however, the softer, chalkier soil of the Cotswolds begins, and arable crops are planted. The change is dramatic, especially in summer, when the linseed comes into flower, covering the land with its delicate lavender veneer. Sometimes, seeking a change from green grass, green trees and green hedges, I ride up to the top of the hill. Looking down across wheat and linseed, I feel like the nomad of the desert who, after saturating vistas of monochrome stone and sand, rests his eyes on the pale blue enamel of a mosque.

English expresses the idea of ploughing in many ways. 'Plough' itself is of Teutonic origin; 'till' also — although Anglo-Saxon 'tielen' originally meant to strive (German *zielen*, to aim), and referred to all kinds of cultivation. In Chaucer's day the verb was 'eren', and some old Wiltshire characters still speak of 'earing' the fields.

This verb is related to the Latin *arare*, to plough, from which we get the word 'arable'. Indeed in every European language there is a verb derived from the root 'ar' and meaning to plough, a fact that has profound implications for our understanding of the pre-history of our continent. We can deduce that the agrarian people who drove the hunter-gatherers out of Europe had a common origin, and that they became powerful with the invention of the plough.

Micah's prophecy of perpetual peace tells us that 'they shall beat their swords into ploughshares'; and the ox-drawn or horse-drawn plough appears in Western painting as an icon of tranquillity – a reminder of the earth's fertility, of the rhythm of the seasons, and of the bond between man and beast. Until the middle of the last century it was normal in Britain for ploughs to be drawn by shire horses, and the image of these beautiful animals as they toiled on the near horizon, the ploughman treading behind, was used repeatedly to raise morale during the dark years of the Second World War. *This* is what we are fighting for, was the message, and – amplified in the paintings of Paul Nash, and the films of Ealing Studios – it was a message that reached every heart.

The horse-drawn plough has not entirely vanished from our continent – you can come across it still in southern Poland and Transylvania. And although it has disappeared from British farming, it has not disappeared from the consciousness of the farmer. Agriculture is one of the few industries in which people adopt new ways of doing things, while striving to immortalize the old. Ceaselessly aiming to save labour and costs, barely able to survive even so, the farmer looks back with intense nostalgia to the older, slower, more earth-bound procedures, not in order to regret them, but in order to celebrate his liberation from their grip. Many farmers keep some memento of the days before the machines took over, when man and beast toiled side by side, when skills were divided and when every task required the cooperation of others. Most of them have never known those days, and freely admit that life then was hard. But they will keep pictures of their farms as once they were, with the horses, the carts, the hay-ricks and the sheep-pens. And when the moment comes, they will bring out an old single plough with knife-blade coulters, they will oil it and grease it, load it onto a trailer and take it to the nearest ploughing competition, there to hitch it to a pair of borrowed shires, and till the stubble in contented competition with their neighbours. For them the plough is a symbol of peace only in this remembered form, the hardship leached away by time.

Those who don't drive horses may still keep an antique tractor, for these too take part in ploughing races, and are lovingly maintained all year for their one moment of glory. Ploughing competitions came into being in the eighteenth century, actively encouraged by that great champion of agriculture, Arthur Young, as a ceremonial endorsement of the farmer's role.[6] They are attended by all the locals, and have their unique festive atmosphere. Many people deliberately dress in dungarees and braces over frayed collarless shirts. Some drink beer out of pewter tankards, in the quantities that were once prescribed by custom. And a queer current of emotion flows over the scene, like the emotion in a theatre. The farmers hupping their sweating horses or crashing the weary gears of paraffin-driven Fords are summoning a way of life that is theirs by right, and which can still be regained through the imagination. And this recreation of a vanished scheme of things, in which life was lived close to the earth, and the farmer was honoured as the guardian of the land and provider of the harvest is, although a holiday recreation, also a real compensation for the trials of modern agriculture. True, it is, like the theatre, a work of the imagination. But consolation from imaginary things is not an imaginary consolation. On the contrary, it is the only real consolation that modern people have.

This work of the imagination does not summon the old procedures only: it summons a gentler way of dealing with the enemy. Top-soil, habitats, waterways, wetlands, gorses, coverts – all are vulnerable to the new machinery, which can sweep them up in an afternoon. Power circles the earth, and just by putting a plug in a socket we call it down from the skies like a thunderbolt. This power brings freedom, and also ignorance – ignorance of our own and others' nature, and of the delicate balance upon which we intrude, by applying to the landscape an energy beyond our means.

If you can uproot a tree by pulling the lever on a JCB, then the rootedness of the tree seems no better than tentative. If you can plough a field in an afternoon merely by keeping a hand on a powered steering wheel, then the link between earth and top-soil seems no stronger than the bond between a butcher's floor and its sawdust. The world falls apart at our approach, as though nothing held it together but gravity. We no longer need to wrestle with nature, to lift or heave or dig. Everything has been re-arranged for our convenience.

From time to time, in this world of mechanism and super-human power, we re-discover the other power that preceded the machine and which will also outlast it – the power that flows through the landscape, and also through us. Digging by hand, lay-ing a hedge with saw and bill-hook, clearing ditches, logging in woodland where only man and horse can find a passage – these experiences measure us against nature and remind us that we are part of it. Although it is the horse who pulls the felled trunks from the copse, you too are strained to the utmost by the task of guid-ing him. Although it is the spade that cuts through the soil and turns it over, you feel the adhesive strength of soil in your muscles.

The new kind of agriculturalist, who sends hired contractors to churn up the land at seed-time and to plunder it at harvest, knows nothing of this. He treats the fields as raw material, to be planted with crops, sold off as top-soil or dug out for gravel as the market requires. Those old tasks of hedging, ditching, coppicing, fencing, and planting covert have no part in his business. The landscape is scooped up by the machines and done away with, all its powers of resistance gone. The small farmer, by contrast, who resides in the land and maintains it as a territory, still feels his tasks in the bone. Power, for him, is not the superhuman power of a vast machine, but the endless heaving and pulling of contrary animals, the fric-tion of tools in the hand, the weight of bales as he swings them into the hay-barn, the obstinate habits of an old-fashioned tractor that will not work the topper. He acquires the shape of his labour – stooped forward like a sickle, ready to address the task in front of him with no power more reliable than his own.

Here and there in the fields or overgrown with brambles along the roadside verges you may still come across rusting pieces of machinery, dating from the transitional period between the horse-drawn plough and the combine harvester – the period celebrated in those war-time books about the countryside, when the tractor had just displaced the horse. These insubstantial skeletons of iron, with iron wheels and smooth iron seats, would clank along behind the tractor, a farmhand perched precariously above their blades and needles, watching the earth as it churned beneath him, pulling levers and pressing pedals, his face dripping with sweat. Now they stand in the nettles and brambles, looking frail and worn like the old men who used to work them. Those old farmhands remember a world in which human will and muscle were matched by nature; in which every action met with an equal and opposite reaction; and in which crops were yielded by the soil only after a year-long fight on terms of complete equality.

Of course, when a labour-saving device is invented, we all begin to use it. But, as we know from the Luddite response to threshing machines in the early nineteenth century, there is always a cost, and this cost is usually borne by those at the bottom of the food chain. And when they bear a cost, so do the rest of us. The man who rattled on that iron seat behind the tractor was the one who dwelt in the land without owning it, whose home was tied to an occupation and who lost everything with his job. Until early in the twentieth century he would be picked up by his employer at a 'hiring fair' in some important market town, and then retained for a year, to be hired again if he was lucky. This insecurity gave the labourer an urgent motive to find the local girl who would argue his case to her farming father, and so provide him with a home. Hence, thanks to the labourer, the gene pool of our farming communities was constantly replenished. The labourer was the leaven in the rural dough, the necessary intruder, the one who brought to rooted communities the habits of elsewhere.

Nothing has affected our farming communities more tragically than the disappearance of the farm labourer, therefore. Losing him, they have lost their lifeline to the outer world. Officially this tragic disappearance has yet to be acknowledged. Right up until our time, the law has made room for the tied agricultural tenancy, while our planners, who on the whole prevent new building in the countryside, continue to make an exception for the 'farm labourer's cottage', now called an 'agricultural worker's home'. One such home was recently built near the neighbouring village of Minety. It has six bedrooms, three bathrooms with jacuzzis, a swimming pool, double garage, external lighting, games room, TV room, tennis court and conservatory, the whole of an unspeakable vulgarity that would look out of place even in the suburbs of Dallas. The businessman who built the 'cottage' has lived there ever since, renting his 'farmhouse' to commuters.

The translation of the farm labourer to the realm of legal fictions does not imply that no-one works on the land. In our part of the world, however, most workers are 'reverse commuters' – people who live in Swindon, where houses are still affordable, and who travel each morning to the fields in their battered pick-ups, passing the sleek Mercedes that are commuting the other way.

Take Roddy, for instance. He began adult life in the army, became a builder, and now works out here, repairing, hedging, dry-stone-walling, growing vegetables, shifting hay and straw. Although he lives in a Swindon council house, Roddy is a countryman through and through, an authority on wildlife and habitats, passionate about birds and wildflowers. He builds in the old way, using chiselled quoins of stone, and has a deep-down knowledge of the soil and its qualities – a knowledge of what can grow in it and of what can be built on top. He could earn twice as much in the town as he earns on the farm; but he would not trade the life of the fields for any building site in Swindon, and is never happier than when working alone and out of sight, strimming around a pond or planting a willow coppice. Always his gun is at his side, and when he passes by in the evening there might be a gift of pigeon breasts or rabbits, or a tale to tell of the crows and magpies – which Roddy hates with a justified venom – now hanging from the oak trees as a warning to their kind.

Roddy is a premodern countryman, transported by economic necessity to the town. Andy, who is half Roddy's age, is a postmodern countryman, but one just as important to our local economy. He comes in the vacations to work as a milkman on Sidney's old farm, occasionally looking after everything – cows, horses, chickens, sheep and a temperamental bull – while Sidney takes his annual holiday. When not making money as a live-in farm labourer, Andy returns to Oxford, where he is studying full-time for a doctorate in microbiology.

Andy loves the country not in the instinctive way of Roddy, but with the anxious curiosity of an anthropologist. Far more important to him than the animals that he tends are the social rituals that surround them. Andy is there at every barbecue and garden party, at every barn dance and pig-roast, at every dog show and at every meet of the beagles or the foxhounds. He is there in the pub of an evening, not imparting knowledge but absorbing it. And when there is a break in his arduous day, you will find him with a book in his hand, studying to acquire from thinking what Roddy knows from life.

People like Roddy and Andy show that, even if the farm labourer is a fiction, the farmer is a fact – an economic fact, but also a social fact, a fact with no equivalent in money. They restore to the farmer some of his damaged self-esteem, as a provider not of food only, but also of jobs, and of the ability to enjoy those jobs regardless of the meagre salary. Of course, it is only odd jobs that our farmers can provide, and for the most part they work alone, like Brueghel's ploughman. Their eyes, like his, are turned to the soil, and their hands, like his, are always driving an implement. Yet, indifferent as Brueghel's ploughman to the world of speculative science, they are not averse to the kind of small-scale but world-transforming innovation of which the plough is the first and as yet hardly surpassed example.

The popular conception of the farmer, as wedded to out-dated ways and surviving in the modern economy only because of subsidies, is in fact the opposite of the truth. From time immemorial farmers have been first among innovators. Agriculture, after all, was the greatest of mankind's discoveries, the decisive move away from subjection to the natural order towards domination of it – in retrospect, the ecologists would have us believe, a mistake, but one that is now irreversible. What makes farmers seem conservative is that they bear the brunt of our collective misfortunes, and must therefore respect the accumulated wisdom of the past. Bad weather, war and pestilence can destroy the harvest, and when one harvest is lost, you must wait a year for the next one. This risk is quite unlike the risks attached to trade and manufacture, and it is not surprising if farmers have had to develop special skills and virtues in order to manage it. They have learned to be patient, to study nature and her ways, to share their knowledge with their neighbours and to help each other in times of trouble. Farmers are quick to sympathize with their rivals in distress. Look back at Virgil's *Georgics*, and you will see how this virtue grows naturally, among those who face the seasons and the elements together.

'Neighbour' derives from two Saxon roots – 'néah' and 'gebúr'. The neighbour is the one who *builds nearby*, and in German the peasant farmer is still a 'Bauer', one who builds. Neighbours do not merely discover the crops best suited to their common soil and the boundaries that lie most firmly on the land that they share: they discover the buildings best adapted to their climate. Their shared discoveries harmonize their seedtimes and their harvests, and lead to harmony of another kind, endowing each region with its aesthetic character and its human face: all of which is summarized in the old word for agriculture, 'husbandry'. Wherever husbandry is still visible – in Provence or Tuscany, in the Welsh borders or the Cotswolds – you will find the urban refugees now settling, entranced by a beauty that was purchased at a cost that they rarely pause to consider and which they will do nothing to supply.

The habit of invention extends to the smallest things. Unlike most people who work in the modern economy, the farmer must acquire a multiplicity of skills if he is to overcome the problems of a normal day: fencing, hedging, milking, herding, tilling and sowing, along with more specialized skills that are trades in themselves. He must be enough of a vet to diagnose his animals' complaints and take the first steps to remedy them. He must be enough of a mechanic to give first aid to the broken-down tractor, to weld the broken harrow, or to fix the hydraulics on a front-loader. He must be enough of a builder to put up a cow-shed or a sheep-pen and enough of a plumber to service the troughs in the field. And he must be constantly on the look-out for new ideas, if he is to obey the cost-cutting imperatives that afflict him.

Much of the farm machinery that we now see in our fields originated as some homely improvisation. Muck-spreaders, furrow presses, hoppers and sprayers are constantly made and re-made to the farmer's special requirements, and every now and then a design is lifted from the farmyard and transcribed on to some manufacturer's drawing board. In no catalogue, however, will you come across a tractor comparable to Marty's – a machine that has grown from the land like an organism in some undiscovered niche. Marty's tractor started life some 20 years ago as a Massey-Ferguson, though the front-loader comes from a Ford, and the cabin from a JCB, welded over the wheels with space for tools and a dog basket. A contraption of steel tubing swings behind, and can be instantly lowered to create a sheep-pen, and raised again with the sheep inside. Bolted to either door are two wheels, on one of which a rope is coiled, on the other a hose. Sheep wire is stored behind the seat, and two slats welded to the roof carry posts and rails for fencing. The grab has been extended almost to the width of our narrow lanes, and its angry-looking tines, as it rounds the corner, send horses and dogs scattering for safety. This is Marty's mobile home and industrial base, his defence against the elements and his armoured sheep protector. Inside its shaking cabin, his senses obliterated by noise, he travels from gate to gate across the fields, his old sheepdog coiled behind him, his face rigid and expressionless like a driver in some children's toy. The creative achievement of a lifetime, Marty's tractor is his one claim to success, a symbol of his will to survive and the mediator between himself and his enemy, the soil.

Marty is a relic of the old rural economy; he owns no land and survives by renting pasture for his sheep, shifting them from field to field around the neighbourhood. He began life as a labourer on a dairy farm, was able to buy a cottage in the days when cottages were affordable, and has botched together a viable life much as he has botched together a functional tractor to share it. He belongs to a social category that has no place in the books of statistics, and no epitaph in the works of academic sociology. He was formed less by human society than by the land, shaped out of clay like Adam. And in this he resembles many others in our neighbourhood.

Beyond the eastern boundary of our farm a few houses lie along a cul-de-sac. The last of them is an old farmhouse that has lost most of its land, and which is maintained in condition of tidy retreat, like a fortress. Here Ben hides away from the world with a few cows, some geese, a mangy old terrier and the woman whom he has never got round to marrying. In the paddock behind the house are two wooden sheds, one of which contains Len's chickens, the other of which we assume contains Len.

Nobody knows where Len came from. Ben, who explains nothing, would certainly not explain Len, though a strange mute attachment can be observed between them which has led to the hypothesis that they are relatives, an hypothesis oddly borne out by their chiming names. Len is small, wiry, with a large jaw stuffed with broken teeth, a stringy moustache and a teddy-boy quiff that shines with what cannot be Brylcreem. He seldom speaks, and is never observed without a blade of grass in his mouth, which he chews vigorously in company or slowly when alone. Once a week he cycles to Malmesbury with a shopping bag hanging from the handle-bars; at other times he patrols the neighbourhood in the company of three Jack Russells, which follow at his heels with down-turned eyes as though indifferent to everything save the boots of their master.

Len, who owns none of this land, nevertheless lives from it. And he lives from it more completely than anyone. In a nearby farmyard there is a patch where he grows his vegetables. No records exist that would justify Len's claim to this patch. But nobody has ever questioned his right to plant and harvest it. Len's chickens forage in the fields and farmyards, but nobody shoos them away. Their eggs exchange for coins that fund Len's weekly shopping trip, and in his wanderings Len picks up scraps of wood, perspex and tarpaulin, which he makes into sheds and hutches. One of these, the result of several months of gathering and cobbling, now houses our chickens. And once a year Len gets the farmer by the main road to pin up a notice, announcing a new rabbit hutch for sale.

One day we awoke to a beautiful autumn morning. Sun and mist were striving to defeat each other, and the trees were cloaked in white and gold. It was a day for blackberrying, and we set off round the farm to fill our baskets from the hedgerows, anticipating that peaceful, evocative and autumnal taste that no fruit from sun-drenched lands can ever rival. To our dismay the ripe blackberries had all disappeared. Only the raw red buttons remained, and we fell to cursing the birds that we have taken such trouble to entice here. Then, at the top of the hill, briefly revealed in a ray of sodden sunlight, we caught sight of Len, chewing contentedly on a blade of grass, and filling his plastic shopping-bag with handfuls of fruit from the hedgerow. We slipped quickly back to the house, reluctant to challenge what was clearly a customary right.

Over breakfast we took stock of our situation. In the vicinity of Len, legal ownership becomes a fiction. But it is not only Len, we realized, who has this effect. Stephen, when he comes to take the silage, pointedly refers to the fields behind the house as Michael's, since Michael, before he sold up, was a *bona fide* farmer, whose family had farmed here for centuries. Stephen's father, who takes the grass keep on the hilltop, has just ploughed and seeded it, not troubling to consult us, since the field will be his henceforth as it was his under the previous owner, and his under the owner before. The other day Stephen's cows appeared unannounced in the fields called Michael's and when we mentioned that we might put horses in Plough Piece it was indicated that this would not be right, since the sheep were due to graze there, having grazed Plough Piece each autumn from the beginning of time.

Other neighbours take charge of adjoining sections of our territory, and obstinately treat the fields as though we had never set foot in them. The land resists our possession and flees back to them, as a dog flees back to its master. Perhaps, if our children take up farming, and their children after them, our claim might at last be acknowledged. For the time being, however, the Scrutons are temporary residents, people whose title depends merely on the accident of legal ownership, and therefore has no authority that could override the immemorial claims of local custom.

Many of the farmers round here are not on speaking terms; but they know who should farm which field, and vigorously defend each others' privileges against the flimsy paper rights of the incomers. When Bert sold up and his farm was bought by Vic the builder, there was a moment of stunned uncertainty, as neighbours who shun each other nevertheless hesitated to lay claim to fields that had never been distributed. Great, therefore, was the scandal when a farmer from the other side of the railway line took the fields before it could be decided who really had a claim to them. For a few days the neighbours were on speaking terms, united in their indignation against the outsider who had usurped their rights – until Mark's cows pushed through the hedge into Chris's hayfield, and things returned to normal.

When it comes to the blackberries in our fields, therefore, our claim will never stand up against Len's in the court of local opinion. The land belongs to us; but Len belongs to the land.

This peculiar intimacy with the soil so removes the farmer from the incomer that the two can barely discuss land without talking at cross-purposes. You look with pride across the field that you own, pleased with its even mantle of grass, its neatly tailored hedgerows and the picturesque grove of ash trees in the corner. Then the farmer comes to rent the field from you, pointing out the acidity of the topsoil, the abundance of holes and pitfalls, the infestation of docks and nettles, the riot of moles, rabbits and badgers, the boggy gateways and the section of broken fence. He explains why no better luck could come your way, than a farmer prepared to tend the place for nothing. In short, he overlays the peaceful view from your window with another and entirely incompatible perspective. Now you see a terrain marked by bitter struggle, fraught with failure, and constantly renewing itself as the implacable enemy of man.

In the course of one such negotiation with our neighbour we came across an argument that we had never heard before, and which has since radically affected our view of the world. The problem with the field under discussion, we were told, was they boopoles. Now some fragments of the old Wiltshire dialect are still in common use: the habit of putting the verb before the subject ('comes the cow'), the lack of declensions ('he tells I about they'), an avoidance of plural verbs ('us is going to market'), a general preference for the present tense. There are even local words, like 'pussyvanting' (mucking around – from French *poursuivant*) and 'shrammed' (frozen). But 'boopole' came as a surprise. I assumed that the offending items were 'boop holes', since apparently they were a great danger to the tractor. I nodded sagely – after all, it would be fatal for someone in my position, after five years pretending to be entirely at one with my surroundings, to confess that I didn't know, of all things, what a boop hole is.

But, as the story unfolded, and it became clear that spraying weren't no good (so 'boo poles', perhaps, like rampant bamboo), that one 'come up sudden right under my feet' (an animal therefore?), that sometimes even they deer is tripped up by boopoles, I began to realize that a boopole is entirely *sui generis*, not observable to someone brought up in the suburbs, or noticeable only in the way that a mouse is noticeable, at the moment when it disappears into its hole. Maybe boopoles are the mysterious things that cause horses to shy for no apparent reason, or dogs to howl in the night. Needless to say I was utterly convinced by my neighbour's reasoning, and agreed to the lowest possible rent.

Sophie and I speculated for a while about the boopoles, and walked around the field in search of them. We discovered a rabbit warren, though no sign of its occupants. There was a large patch of nettles, and one or two dips in the ground. But nothing that deserved the name 'boopole'. We listed boopoles among the other unsolved mysteries of Sunday Hill Farm – as immune to rational enquiry as the nocturnal creaking in the attic, as the piles of horsehair by the pond or the sudden sighting one afternoon of a blue bedraggled cockatoo.

And then one day Sophie came running into the house in a state of alarm. 'Come quickly,' she cried, 'there's something in the barn, something big; maybe a boopole.'

The cows had left weeks ago for the fields. There was nothing in the barn save discarded furniture, with a sofa and a heap of curtains piled on its back. But something was definitely moving behind the sofa, shoving massively against it and causing the curtains to wobble and totter. There was a scraping and grunting, as though the creature were building a nest there, or trying to tunnel into the concrete floor. Clearly I should have to confront it. Questions that I should have asked our neighbour crowded into my mind. Are boopoles herbivores or carnivores? Do they have teeth at all, or on the contrary do they merely chew the cud like cows? Are they shy of human beings or aggressive when cornered? Here was my ultimate encounter with the mystery of rural life, and it was clearly dangerous.

Armed with an old kitchen chair, which I reckoned could be set down between me and the boopole and interpreted either as a defence against aggression or as a friendly invitation to discuss things, I approached the tumult. Boopoles are obviously large, I realised, as large as a Great Dane or a Gloucester Old Spot. I steeled myself for our meeting with the thought that large animals are on the whole more gentle than small ones. But I was not in the least prepared for the sight that met me as I rounded the pile of furniture, and turned to confront the intruder.

Lying against the sofa, on a patch of straw that had been swept up there, was a Friesian bull, his cloven hoofs jutting from under his belly, his melancholy eyes turned upwards to observe me. He uttered a long disconsolate bellow, struggled to his feet, thought better of it, and sank down again with a grunt. It was the bull from Clitchbury Farm, wandering again, as he wanders each summer. He looked at me with such an air of vulnerable loneliness that I began to apologize for disturbing him. Was he comfortable there? Was there anything he needed? Some hay perhaps? A drink of water?

I was treating the bull as townies do, both petting him and fearing him. I was doing everything to ensure that our relations ended in disaster. This Mick, the owner, explained to me when he came on the scene. 'He wants a good kick and a wallop behind, and a sight of they cows down the road there.' Mick had soon rustled him out into the farmyard, pointed him in the direction of his herd, and sent him with a slap along the road. Bulls, I recognized, really are boopoles: mysteries that townies will never decipher. The word has now entered our vocabulary, as a generic name for those aspects of clayland life that baffle us. I learned in due course that the word is not 'boopole' at all but 'bull-paul', a dialect term (maybe French *'boule-polle'*) denoting clumps of reed grass that harden like ant-heaps over clay, forming obstacles that are impossible to level without the plough. At Sunday Hill Farm, however, our obstacles are not physical but metaphysical, barriers between us and the soil. And all of them are boopoles.

2

Our People

The Somerford Show has been in existence for 105 years. It takes place in a large tree-lined field, overlooked by the grey-stone tower of Great Somerford Church, which rises on a knoll to the south of it. In past years, the field has been vacated the day before the show by the cows that normally pasture in it, and the avoidance of cow-pats has been part of the fun. Hygiene regulations now tell us that the public must not be admitted to a field with cow-pats. In order to fulfil his communal duty, therefore, the farmer has had to suffer a substantial economic loss. The unpredictable costs of needless regulations are invariably borne, in this way, by small communities like ours.

By the time it occurs, the show has been the focus of several months of social activity, with committees, dinners, after-dinner speeches, and a re-run of last year's quarrels and reconciliations. The day itself is centred on equestrian events, with jumping, driving and judging of working hunters. Our neighbour's four-year-old son Jack enters the competitions for ponies on a lead-rein. He and Jill, his farming mother, have worked for hours grooming and polishing – not the pony only, but Jack too. This amiable but normally far from elegant urchin appears in tweed jacket, jodhpurs, shirt, tie and polished boots, to sit on his pony in a line and be judged. The judge is an old military man with an honourable limp, dressed in rat-catcher and bowler; the ponies are led by ladies in long dresses, straw hats and gloves. All, in their way, are being judged. And marks are given for smartness, discipline, good manners, control, demeanour, and style – values that are decidedly politically incorrect, but which are the stuff of our society. By competing with each other the children learn to emulate the virtues that we hope they

23

will one day acquire, and the sensible improvement to Jack's manners lasts for all of five minutes afterwards.

The children's event is succeeded by others, all equally incorrect: the driving competition, in which ladies in elaborate Victorian costumes manifest their skills with whip and rein; the show of hunters, invoking the discipline and danger of the field; and the display of hounds – representing what is still the most important of our social institutions – with the huntsman blowing his horn at the head of them. All the farmers and their spouses are present. Some are dressed in tweeds and long dresses, having been invited to the judges' lunch, an event whose social importance is measured by the fact that so many are excluded from it. Vegetables, handicrafts, jams, pickles and cakes are displayed in a large marquee, all graded according to merit. There is also a competition for the best bale of hay, eliciting pride in a crop that is both vital to our local ecology and threatened by the new forms of agribusiness.

'Good hay, sweet hay, hath no fellow,' says Bottom, and there is not a herbivore who would dissent from that judgement. Grass is the anchor of the food chain, and the saying of the prophet Isaiah, that 'all flesh is grass', conveys a profound truth about the human condition, expressed in another way by Evan Eisenberg: 'the basis of human proliferation is not our own seed but the seed of grasses'.[7] Silaging – which involves cutting grass early, wrapping it in air-tight plastic, and leaving it to ferment into a rich pudding of proteins – has made grass-lands dependable, since they can be harvested with only the shortest spell of sunshine. But it has also radically changed them, both visually and ecologically. The first cut of silage occurs before the young of ground-nesting birds have flown, before leverets have become knowledgeable, before snakes have sloughed off their winter skins or deer have weened their calves. When first carried out on an ancient meadow, the result is carnage. Moreover, this early cutting favours grass that spreads rapidly through its roots, over the varieties that are more dependent on seeding. The combined effect of early cutting and fertilization is to introduce a monoculture of rye-grass. The swaying, winsome, multifarious threads disappear from the landscape, and with them the birds that depended on their seeds, and the creatures that nested beneath them.

When H. Rider Haggard, author of *King Solomon's Mines* and that astonishing tour-de-force *She*, decided to settle, it was on a clay farm in Norfolk, not much bigger than Sunday Hill Farm. There – subsidized by his royalties – he devoted himself to turning the sticky soil to profit: draining lowlands, clearing ditches and re-seeding pastures. Here is the grass mixture that he planted: fiorin, meadow foxtail, crested dogtail, rough cocksfoot, hard fescue, tall fescue, sheep's fescue, meadow fescue, rye grass, greater birdsfoot trefoil, common yellow clover, timothy, rough stalked meadow grass, alsike clover, red clover, white clover, with four deep-rooting herbs to push through the clay: chicory, burnet, lucerne and yarrow.[8] The contrast with modern ways is eloquent. When our farmers re-seed a field they lightly turn the surface, using a roto-vator rather than a deep-coultered plough for fear of turning up the clay, and then scatter unmixed Italian rye grass, which will give two cuts of silage, whatever the weather, and which will therefore make the pasture pay. In the face of this aesthetic and ecological disaster, our competition for the best bale of hay is both a lingering backward glance to the world of Rider Haggard and also a collective bid to save our meadows, by those condemned to destroy them.[9]

Somerford show is a collective and ceremonial repossession of our spot of earth. Our hard-working neighbours assemble here to enjoy the loyalties, hierarchies and formalities that define their way of life. The dress codes, the ponies and traps, the handicrafts, even the over-sized vegetables and the knobbly fruit-cakes, are unmis-takeably English and unashamedly proud of it. And our neigh-bours assemble to display these things in full knowledge that all of this – not just livestock farming and hunting, but all the habits that are here recollected in tranquillity – are under threat. Seeing our people in their natural and self-made social environment, you know that they are entitled to it, as entitled as Brueghel's plough-man to his plot on nowhere's edge.

Nor is this real society weaponless in the face of local misfor-tune. Consider the Ames's, who have farmed in our valley for sev-eral generations. Old Larry Ames, great-grandfather of Jack, was a farm labourer until the age of 40, when he fell while stacking straw and broke his spine. He has lived for 35 years in a wheel-chair, the lower half of his body paralysed. Each evening his daughter Margaret comes to his cottage, and drives Larry to her husband's ramshackle farm, where he spends the night. In the morning he plays with his great-grandchildren (who love him all the more for his wheels) before being taken back home for the day. Larry has never complained; it would never cross his mind to sue the owner of that strawstack, nor would he expect buildings and facilities to be adapted to his disability. He is always cheerful, suffering now from painful illnesses but coming through with a smile on his face to take his natural place in the community, which is that of a proud great-grandad. Many people visit old Larry, saying 'I will cheer him up'; but when they leave him wreathed in smiles you know that their real reason for visiting Larry was to be cheered up themselves.

Margaret lost her young son in another accident: rather than retreat in bitterness, she looks after the children of neighbours, ours included, and loves them through their early years. Larry's sons operate our local business, dealing in hay and straw; his one surviving grandson works on Margaret's farm. They are the core of the local economy. Even in these difficult times, when nothing can be legally slaughtered or sold except at a cost calculated to destroy such anachronistic people, the Ames's continue to produce pork and bacon, sausages, eggs, and poultry. One look at the courtyard of their farm, with its riot of children, dogs, chickens, ducks, ponies, porkers and a superannuated cow, is enough to tell you that these are hardened criminals.

Their social life only confirms the impression. Margaret cooks Sunday dinner for those farmers who now live alone. Her family stage pig-roasts and birthday parties; and at the meet of foxhounds they are there, handing out the port and sausages, Jack on his tiny pony swearing vengeance against the murderer of his granny's chickens. They quarrel with their neighbours, because that is what real and living people do. But they also make up with them, and would never dream of taking their complaints to any higher tribunal than local gossip.

Like many of our people who have gone through a time of real religious need, Margaret became a Roman Catholic. Her reaching for a church that beckons from another sphere illustrates the dwindling role of religion in the life of our community. The Ames children are married and baptized in church, and they themselves are buried there, since that is what decency requires. But formal worship is no part of their routine. At the same time they display, in their unassuming way, the Christian ideal of 'witness'. Every encounter with old Larry is a withering reproach to selfishness. His

angelic face tells us that we are commanded by duty, and rewarded by love. The Ames's are happy because they do not complain,
because they get willing help from others to whom they offer help
in turn, because they refuse to depend on the meddlers and believe
that neighbourliness and self-reliance are inseparable aspects of a
single way of life. Such people fill the reservoir of social emotion
that the state depletes, and show that charity begins at home and
also ends there.

Our health service and our education system were once widely
admired. In both spheres the state expropriated an accumulation
of private capital, in the form of buildings, services, equipment,
expertise and – most important of all – moral commitment and the
people who embodied it. The state did not produce those things.
They were the legacy of philanthropy, patriotism and local loyalties, of the kind that feed from sacrificial lives like Margaret's. But,
for a glorious moment, before the rot of centralization set in, the
state enhanced this private legacy, supplementing it with public
funding and well-meant schemes for social justice.

Among our people you can still find the human capital from
which the health service began. Mrs Weld, our District Nurse, is a
singular example. A farmer's daughter, now in her early fifties and
with a daughter of her own, Mrs Weld (for so, out of respect for
her vocation, is she addressed) enters each house on her stocky legs
with the same bum-slapping good humour with which a farmer
enters the milking shed. Patients visibly brighten at her approach,
for she radiates competence and interest, while at the same time
implying that she shares the sufferer's inner knowledge of his ailments, and feels privileged to belong to the drama.

The institution of District Nurse has its roots in Victorian philanthropy, and in the example set by Florence Nightingale. But it
has developed through the NHS in a new and wholly benevolent
way, so as to enable the chronically sick to live comfortably at
home. (Though it should be said that there is a charge for the
District Nurse, and her comforts are real partly because they are
paid for.) Without the District Nurse hospitals would be more
crowded than they are, and many sick and disabled people would
be condemned to live as social outcasts. Even old Larry Ames, who
is as deeply immersed in society as an invalid can be, has come to
depend upon Mrs Weld. He waits for her in his wheelchair every
Monday morning, preparing for the moment when she enters the

kitchen with a loud 'Good Morning!' to begin their habitual dialogue. Larry pretends that last week's sore is no longer troubling
him, she tut-tuts at his futile bravery, and implies that she felt the
sore already, just as soon as she came through the door. And then,
having re-affirmed the terms of their relationship, she turns the
conversation to the business of the farm.

Mrs Weld is neat and clean in a motherly way; but obsessive
hygiene is no part of her style. She attends to Larry as she might to
a horse or a cow; and those who have seen a conscientious farmer
dressing the wound of an animal will know the extent to which
robust reassurance and real gentleness can coexist in a single
gesture. Larry loathes the disinfected atmosphere of hospitals; he
dreads the crises that take him – never, alas to the sweet cottage
hospitals in Malmesbury or Cirencester – but always to the
bleached morgue of Swindon, with its flourescent corridors and
room upon room of sterile isolation. With Mrs Weld, however,
Larry is both literally and figuratively at home. They talk of the
land, the people and the farms round about. She gives a full report
of the hunt, conjuring the fields, woods and ditches that Larry has
not seen for years, but which he visits now in imagination, as
though carried on his companion's firm, strong legs.

Mrs Weld's presence reassures because it normalizes. Larry's
sickness, being the foundation of this friendship between two old-
fashioned rustic characters, ceases to be a disability and becomes a
natural event in the farmyard. And when the nurse leaves the
house Larry gives her a matey goodbye, implying that he receives
her visits as ordinary social calls, with no special purpose beyond
the tie of neighbourly affection.

For a long while afterwards nevertheless, Larry remains smiling
and sociable in his wheelchair. And Mrs Weld too seems refreshed
by her visits. Her patients normalize her way of life just as she
normalizes their illnesses. Chronically sick people need such contact
far more than they need specialist treatment, and to them the
District Nurse is worth a hundred consultants.

Rural life is replete with these rugged individuals because it
contains the forms of life that create them. Our 'little platoons'
shape people to each other, endowing them with the psychic cor-
regations that slot together in times of need. 'Social exclusion',
when it occurs, arises by an invisible hand, a side-effect of the global economy as it sweeps across our pastures. And even then, the

term is a misnomer. Consider the case of Vince, 14 years old, an inveterate truant, who has now been excluded from our local school, to which he reacted as you or I would react to false imprisonment. Vince cannot read or write, and lives with his equally illiterate parents in a cottage by the railway. Vince's parents were farmers, and their parents before them. In the days when milking was profitable, when meat was bought and sold at market and when governments respected the local economy, knowing that when push comes to shove (as it did in 1939) we all depend on it, their tiny farm of pasture, adjacent to ours, kept the family alive. But in an economy based on paperwork, the hereditary dyslexia that has dogged Vince's family from generation to generation finally condemned them to ruin.

Visits from the school inspector and the social worker notwithstanding, Vince is content with his lot. Moreover, unlike the majority of teenage boys in our local school, he has a clear vision of his future career, and skills that amply fit him to pursue it. For Vince wants to be a pest control officer. He identifies instinctively with wild animals, being one of them himself. He knows their habits and their habitats, how to capture them, care for them and also kill them. With his eager weasel face and wiry limbs he will corner the most determined rat and despatch it instantly. He has a menagerie of birds and rodents, including four barn owls that he has bred himself, a pair of ferrets, and a collection of lurchers and terriers, some of them on 'loan' from the gypsies. He can coax owls and hawks into any territory and provide them with a nesting place. And his favourite occupation after dark is to borrow a farmer's shotgun and go out 'lamping' in the fields.

Lamping involves dazzling a wild animal with a powerful torch and then shooting between its eyes. Such a practice is in the highest degree unsporting, indiscriminate in targeting young and old, hale and sick, suckling mothers and sterile grandads. Nevertheless the farmer who lends his gun to Vince does so because he sees Vince as an immovable member of our rural community, with a hereditary right to territory, regardless of the niceties of ownership. He knows that Vince is a poacher by instinct, who kills quickly and cleanly, not so as to enjoy the suffering but so as to belong to the night and to the animals who move in it.

By day Vince lavishes on his menagerie all the care and affection that he banishes from his nocturnal psyche. For this too is the poacher's way. He is constantly learning about animals, constantly finding new ways of using them and enhancing their powers. The money Vince earns from rat-catching or rabbit-poaching he spends on food for his dogs and ferrets. If they are content, then so too is Vince. Ralph Touchett, in Henry James's *The Portrait of a Lady*, remarks: 'I call people rich when they're able to meet the requirements of their imagination.' By that standard Vince is the richest boy in our village.

The farmer who protects Vince is a Christian, who knows that the boy has been violent at school not because he is a villain but because his soul was not shaped to pass through such a mill. He sees Vince less as a noble savage than as an unconverted heathen. And in doing so he extends to Vince the real spirit of community, accepting the boy's love of the wild as a tribute to the Creator – a tribute that has yet to form itself as faith.

It is unlikely, however, that it will do so. One of the most striking features of our people is their ability to combine Christian customs with pagan beliefs. All over our part of Wiltshire, in every village and hamlet, sometimes even standing alone at a crossroads, you will come across Methodist chapels – bare Georgian meeting-rooms in brick or Victorian shacks of slatboard and corrugated iron, with perfunctory gothic windows and a back yard of rampant shrubs. The Georgian buildings survive from an intense spell of evangelism, led by John Cennick and George Whitefield, disciples of Wesley, in the mid-eighteenth century – an evangelism that led Cennick to bring the Moravian Church to East Tytherton (where their place of worship still functions) and also to Malmesbury. During the nineteenth century the farmers drifted back into the Anglican fold, where faith and piety, which are hard to combine with a seven-day week, are less obviously needed. The days of evangelism appeared then like a global storm which had blown itself out, leaving foreign churches and foreign customs scattered across the landscape in postures of death. By the mid-nineteenth century religion was probably in no better shape in the claylands than in the Hampshire parish of Eversley, where Charles Kingsley was appointed Rector in 1844:

> *The church ... was nearly empty before he came in 1844. The farmers' sheep, when pasture was scarce, were turned into the neglected churchyard. Holy Communion was celebrated only*

three times a year; the communicants were few; the alms were collected in an old wooden saucer. A cracked kitchen basin inside the font held the water for Holy Baptism...[10]

A hundred years ago, however, farm prices were collapsing, the indigenous population was drifting to the towns, and the farmers had no voice in Parliament. They again deserted the established church for its Wesleyan rival, not so much because they had regained the evangelical fervour of the 1750s, as from a sense that the Anglican Church no longer spoke for them. John Wesley's God, they were soon reminded, was inseparable from the puritanical habits of his suburban worshippers – habits that don't last long in the countryside – and the non-conformist faith was no sooner resumed than lost. Almost all our Methodist chapels now stand empty and unvisited, unless they have been acquired as second homes. Nor has the Church of England regained its congregation. Farmers now look up to Heaven in tongue-tied puzzlement, wondering whether Nobodaddy is there.

The distance between the Anglican church and the farmer is never more apparent than at the event that traditionally united them: harvest. *Haerfest* – the festival of cropping – names a time of relief and celebration, when nature is seen at its kindliest, and the stores are finally brought home. The Reformation, which forbade the celebration of saints and their gaudy holidays, permitted the Harvest Festival, for it was a spontaneous recognition of man's dependence, and of the goodness of God. When I was young, not only churches, but schools, village halls and hospitals were decked out at harvest time with sheaves of corn, piles of apples, pears and marrows, trays of beans and carrots, as each family vied with its neighbour to give proof of horticultural skill. Although my family could provide nothing save a few roots from the allotment and a tin of baked beans, I remember the Harvest Festivals of childhood as occasions when God seemed suddenly more real, more manifest, more part of the landscape, than in those remote Biblical stories and moralizing sermons that made the Protestant religion such a burden of insufferable clap-trap to a sceptical child. Even the old German hymn – 'We plough the fields and scatter/The good seed on the land' – seemed to capture the truth of our condition, as we stood in our school assembly, contemplating a Wonderloaf on a bed of straw. We still sing that famous hymn in the claylands, but the produce on display in our church bears little relation to the crops that lie in the fields. Nor is there any farmer present to illustrate our song. We gather to celebrate a virtual harvest, disconnected from the fields outside.

In its own, quiet, embarrassed way, however, the Anglican religion goes on, maintaining churches that it cannot fill but which keep patient vigil in the countryside, awaiting the Prodigal's return. The Anglican church survives today for the very same reason that it has always survived, namely because it is a monument to the language and culture of the English people, an affirmation of the land, and a guardian of the dead who lie there. Of course, it is also a Christian church, with a message of redemption. But it couches this message in an idiom of safety and homecoming. The old Prayer Book tells us that 'we are his people and the sheep of his pasture', and that 'we have erred and strayed from his ways like lost sheep'. Its language and thought are pastoral, and its message of redemption is also a covert affirmation of the rural life from which we have been sundered. That is why country churches have such appeal to the modern traveller, who steps for a moment from his car, creaks open the old wooden door, and sniffs that curious smell of dried flowers and polished brass which is the smell of God at home in England.

English churches tell of a people who preferred seriousness to doctrine, and routine to enthusiasm – people who hoped for immortality but did not really expect it, except as a piece of English earth. The walls are covered with discreet memorials, placing the dead at the same convenient distance that they occupied when living. The pews are hard, uncomfortable, designed not for lingering but for moments of penitence and doubt. The architecture is noble but bare and quiet, without the lofty aspiration of the French Gothic, or the devotional intimacy of an Italian chapel. More prominent than the altar are the lectern, the pulpit, the choir-stalls and the organ. For this is a place of singing and speaking, in which Biblical English passes the lips of people who have believed that holy thoughts need holy words, words somehow removed from the business of the world, like gems lifted from a jewel box and then quickly returned to the dark.

Such a church depends vitally on music, and church music depends in turn upon the organ. But many of the organs in our villages are now silent. One nearby parish even has a choir, properly robed and entering in procession, but with no-one to accompany their singing. Our nearest church was without a regular organist until I volunteered for the position, and no sooner had I done so than requests came from places of worship in the neighbourhood, many of which had been without music for a decade or more.

The rural England described by Thomas Hardy, George Gissing and Flora Thompson was full of music. Not church music only, but folk song and dance, brass bands, orchestras, choral societies. Every neighbourhood had its circles devoted to chamber music, parlour songs and glees. Families had their repertoires of ballads, carols, ditties, and part songs; people would sing at home while they worked or whistle like piccolos in the fields. The upright piano was a status symbol: everyone aspired to own one. There were piano teachers in the villages and children would sing round the piano at the village school, learning folk songs and ballads and acquiring the musical culture of their ancestors.

This habit of music-making has not entirely died in the clay-lands, nor are young people averse to acquiring it. Children in our neighbourhood learn serious instruments (piano, violin, French horn, flute, oboe and many more); teenagers sing in choirs and play in bands; there are concerts and recitals in which near-professionals wrestle with some taxing repertoire. Our village has a brass band; the nearby market town of Wootton Bassett boasts a symphony orchestra. Jamie Cullum, the sensational jazz pianist, is a graduate of Malmesbury jazz club. And behind all this music-making, hidden but known to everyone, there was Ron.

Ron gave lessons in brass and woodwind to children in our village and taught music in the local schools. Fourteen years ago, recognizing that the higher purpose of a musical education is not to play alone but to play together, he put together a band for his pupils. He did not at first expect more than a handful of them to join. But so entranced were the children by the experience that the band quickly expanded to an orchestra, now divided into a junior and senior section, with a full strength of 70 players. Learning an instrument ceases to be a chore, when the reward is playing together: 'I' and 'thou' are transcended, and a collective 'we' replaces them. So argued the Viennese sociologist Alfred Schutz, who added that the 'we' of music causes us to move together with a common will.[11]

Ron was a product of the Brass Band movement, which for two centuries has united our country in a common musical culture.

And he illustrates what is precious in that culture: namely, its ability to combine genuine musicianship with an inclusive repertoire and an easy-going taste. A concert by the Four Winds Concert Band (so it is named) might include film music from *Titanic*, a symphony by Haydn, snippets of Andrew Lloyd Webber, and a selection of Christmas carols. Like many bandmasters, Ron was an arranger and adapter, who shaped the music to the players, just as he shaped the players to the music. He illustrates the truth so ponderously explored by Alfred Schutz: his band is a community, advancing from 'I' to 'we' through music.

In adapting Haydn's *Surprise Symphony* for the combined forces at his disposal – from the 12-year-old violinist to the 40-year-old parent on the tuba – Ron's musicianship was severely tested. But it worked; the players loved it, and the concerts were a success. For many years Ron took the Band to play aboard the QE2 in Southampton. But its main role in our community, apart from that of instilling the love of music in the young, has been to play in village halls and draughty churches, to audiences that are all the more delighted for the fact that they recognize each face among the players. Ron's sudden death, aged 45, has left a painful wound; but the band lives on, and the wound will be healed by music.

Ron's function was once fulfilled by the village organist, who was frequently a paid employee of the parish. The organist was also a teacher, choir-master, organiser, maybe an amateur composer of hymns, whose tunes would take the name of the place where they were composed; he would have a deep love of the instrument and of the repertoire bequeathed by the great keyboard composers, treating the organ as our nearest equivalent to the voice of God.

I learned to play the instrument from such a devoted organist: a small, quiet man who wore a tweed suit even in summer and who lived alone with his ageing mother. If he spoke it would be of music and, like Dylan Thomas's Organ Morgan, he acknowledged no authority besides Bach. He would never touch the organ without first wiping his fingers on a handkerchief, and he prefaced his performances with a moment of reverential silence as though summoning the notes from on high. His life had been pledged, like the life of a monk, and the expression on his face as he performed was one of religious transfiguration. And since I was a boy like any other, who came to my lessons with dirty fingers and dirty thoughts, he put me off the organ for 40 years.

At the end of those 40 years, when I felt mysteriously prompted to volunteer, I was relieved to discover that the little organ in All Saints, Garsdon, has one keyboard, no pedals and only three stops. An electric bellows fills it with air, and the mellow old pipes sing with an almost human music. Sometimes there is a power cut, and George, the most robust member of the congregation, goes behind the instrument to pump away at the hand-bellows that are still attached to it. And this tumultuous exercise, which I channel with my fingers into thin sweet pipes of sound, emerges from the organ dissolved in music, as the soul of the believer is dissolved in God.

Our hymnal is the one edited by Vaughan Williams, who was born in these parts and who composed here the greatest of modern hymns: Down Ampney ('Come Down O Love Divine'), named after the nearby village where Vaughan Williams's father was vicar. VW was not a believer, but a fellow-traveller of the Christian faith who perceived the deep spiritual unity between the Anglican Church and the national culture that he did so much to revive, and that he tried to epitomize in his dramatization of Bunyan's *Pilgrim's Progress*. His hymn tunes are meticulous in their respect for the spirit of Christian England, and are incomparable adjuncts to the Book of Common Prayer. Our congregation still relies on that remarkable book, recognizing that words don't become holy through being repeated, but get repeated because they are holy. We belong to the marginalized set of 'Old Believers', who look on with bewilderment as the Anglican Church presents ever trendier, ever more secular 'alternatives' to the only sources of authority that it has ever had.

There is a special reason for retaining the old rituals. 'We have in England,' wrote Addison, 'a particular bashfulness in everything that regards religion.' At the time (nearly three centuries ago) Addison was our local MP. And his words are still true of the villages around Malmesbury. In our church, armoured by the Prayer Book and cheered on by the hymns, we maintain the distance without which English people cannot be at ease with one another or with God. That is why the village churches of England make such a deep impression on the traveller. God has been in residence here, has moved with stiff English decorum around these light-filled spaces, and played the part of host to generations of people whose shyness He shares. By following the ancient forms, you understand the lasting English need for an established religion – a religion that mutters in the background, demanding neither passionate belief nor strenuous observance, but in some mysterious way consecrating the land.

Nevertheless, the voice of prayer sounds faintly now in our landscape. Most of our farmers would not be seen dead in church, even if they are always seen dead there. But while their ancestors lie buried in the churchyard, they themselves usually stop off at church on their way to the crematorium. Seventy per cent of our British dead are disposed of in this way – a proportion exceeded only by the Czechs. Our farmers no longer wish to be part of the soil they have tended, but prefer, like the majority, to vanish without trace. As Ken Worpole has argued, this vast change in our funerary habits indicates a deep transformation in the collective psyche. The British people have been unsettled, and farmers too. Their funerals used to express their attachment to the homeland and to the spirits that dwell in it. Now they are conceived as flights from the earth, final escapes into nowhere.[12]

The obligatory stopover at the church vastly complicates my duties as an organist, since it involves playing the random snatches of pop song and music-hall kitsch that the relatives associate, for whatever reason, with the dear departed. But it also underlines the significance for our people of the Anglican Church. It is a sign of their ancient settlement, and its rites of passage mark their brief time on earth. The liturgy, the prayers, the hymns, the metrical psalms – all are only vaguely, though poignantly, remembered, like the perfume of an aunt long dead. But the church's presence is always assumed, as durable as law and, like law, mysterious and intangible.

Hence the belief persists among the older farmers that bride and groom are not truly married until the church has said so. Weddings are the moments when a community defines itself for the next generation. The marriage ceremony is the public endorsement of a private choice, and the private endorsement of a public culture. If you want to know how a community views itself, therefore, you should take a look at its weddings. This is what Philip Larkin did, in a famous poem. And 'The Whitsun Weddings' offers a poignant insight into the English as they were in 1958, before sexual intercourse began.

Half a century of sexual intercourse has irreversibly changed things, and weddings don't happen often now in our local church.

Young people leave the district before they get married. Or, if they settle nearby, it is often because they have obtained social housing, which is the only housing that young people in the countryside can afford. There is a well-established route to social housing, which is to get pregnant without getting hitched. The welfare system is an integral part of the household budget, and the background condition from which the new kinds of household emerge. This does not mean that our locals are 'welfare scroungers' but rather that they are rational beings, who do those things that are subsidized, and avoid those things – like marriage – the costs of which are borne entirely by those who undertake them. Moreover they are responding in their own way to a culture that repudiates long-term commitments and pours scorn on the ceremonies that endorse them.

The consequences of this for a settled farming community are extremely serious. When durable marriages give way to fungible partnerships, the family farm will die. The vaporization of the marriage vow is, it seems to me, a far more important factor in the farming crisis than any change in agricultural policy or the balance of trade. Ten years ago, when I first subscribed to *Farmers' Weekly*, I would peruse the lonely hearts column with wonder and amusement, since the only thing offered there was marriage, and the only vital statistics mentioned as an inducement concerned the number of acres, the nature and size of the herd, the qualities of the soil, the yield of crops and – just occasionally – a catalogue of the available machinery. *Farmers' Weekly*'s lonely hearts column has since shrunk to a tiny corner, offering postmodern relationships and eager ladies from Thailand.

Nevertheless, perhaps because of a residual tenderness towards the family farm, the children of farmers have a tendency to creep back into the fold of once customary morality. If there are bridesmaids at our weddings, they are children of the bride, and the families who attend the ceremony may be meeting for the first time. But these departures from tradition serve merely to emphasize the orthodoxy of what remains. Weddings between the children of farmers are invocations of the English divinity, solemnizations of a union in which three people are joined: man, wife and England, all three of them crippled by shyness. They are profoundly unsettled bows towards the God of settlement, a last ditch attempt not to be gathered up in the global maelstrom and blown away to nowhere.

There is one local church activity, however, in which the Anglican shyness is transcended and settlement loudly reaffirmed: bell-ringing. Ezra Pound saw bell-ringing as proof that the English are devoid of music. What other people could devote so many hours to producing so cacophonous a sound, while convincing themselves that God enjoys it? Change ringing was introduced in the seventeenth century, when our native tradition of religious music was being ruthlessly destroyed. It is therefore tempting to believe that this art – which is no more than a relentless permutation of the diatonic scale – is part of a deliberate attempt to obliterate the memory of music. More atmospheric by far is the single chime of the Catholic chapel, the gong of the Buddhist temple or the voice of the muezzin from the minaret.

That is not how Ian sees things. Having been brought up in the Anglican Church, which he has served as teacher in a village school, and then, in retirement, as churchwarden, Ian regards campanology as a sacred rite. It is not so much a way of bringing the people to church, in Ian's thinking, as a way of bringing church to the people. The bells transform the landscape, with the message of God's love radiating over hill and dale, making the country its own.

Ian's feelings are perhaps unusual. Mike, who is half Ian's age, joined our local team for company, and because he needs to exercise his arms after a week's paper-pushing for the District Council. However, what began as a hobby soon became a vocation. Yet more devoted to the cause is Sandra, who together with her father runs the family farm at the bottom of our road. These are first among our local campanologists, and they form a cross-section of rural society as it is today: farming, teaching, and the outreach of the ever-expanding bureaucracy form the core occupations of our community.

To make bells ring in sequence it is not the ear but the eye that must be trained, since the sound of your bell reaches you a second or more after you have pulled on the rope. Rope-sight, as it is called, comes after years of practice, in which you stand among sweating fellows, enjoying a strange community of exertion translated into a faint spiritual echo in the air above, a wild but distant tintinnabulation like a witches' sabbath. People are exalted by this ritual, as by a sacred dance, and if you meet Ian, Sandra and Mike in the pub after practice, you are always uplifted by the sight of their triumphant smiles as they discuss the mishaps of the day.

Mishaps there are, for bells are dangerous. They can sear your hands, slip your discs and sprain your muscles. If they swing full circle they can break their stays and cart you up to the ceiling, sending you crashing unconscious to the floor. And, because of the obsessive nature of the sport, which tempts the ringers to try change after change until the whole repertoire has been accomplished, bells tire you out to the point where mistakes are ever more likely, and ever more difficult to correct. Our local church has only six bells, and therefore 720 changes – a blessed relief, I thought, in the days when I agreed with Pound. Malmesbury has eight, which gives 40,320 changes, while in Cirencester there is an inexhaustible but exhausting peal of ten.

All this Ian tells me as he downs his fourth pint of bitter. Ian's small, quiet face radiates inner satisfaction, and his grey eyes look not outwards at me but inwards, to the ritual that occupies his waking hours. When he goes on holiday, he tells me, it is to some English village known for its peal of bells, where he can insert himself into the local team and get to know their instruments. For each bell is different, and when the founders emboss them with some mystical inscription, it is by way of recognizing that bells have a sound, a movement, a life and a soul of their own.

And another thing, Ian adds. Ringers are believers; but they don't believe as vicars do. Theirs is not an orthodox, still less a theological faith. It is like a cult, a direct appeal to local saints, in which you wrench and tug at your protectors until they do your bidding. Ringers are the last true Catholics within the Protestant Church, in league with their local saints and appealing to them for daily miracles. The bells are there to bless the landscape and to bring God to the people in a humanized form. And that is why, until the time of the Oxford movement, when joy was once again accepted in the Anglican Church, there was such conflict between ringers and priests. Ringers often locked the Rector out of church so that they could praise God in their own high-spirited way, and the clergy denounced the occupants of the belfry as drunken pagans, who would ring for the devil if he paid more than the church.

So Ian says, and Mike and Sandra smile delightedly. But this is Ian's sixth pint of bitter and I relay the scepticism of Pound. 'Ours is not music to be listened to,' he retorts, calling for his seventh pint, 'but a sound to be heard, like the wind in the trees or the babble of a stream. And you should be grateful. When the bells are ringing you don't hear the motorway; you're not bothered by car alarms and tractors. We restore the tranquillity of the landscape, that's what we do. Think of us,' he adds, with a sudden laugh, 'as a kind of silence.'

And there is a truth in Ian's words. English bells are not music, nor are they merely noise. They are the voice of the landscape, recalling us to another, slower, quieter way of living.[13] Their clamour is merely the energetic outrush of a sound that softens as it washes across the countryside, to lap against the farmsteads with the same soporific muttering as the grunts and moos within. By flowing into every yard, the bells affirm the landscape as a common territory, whose boundaries are permeable to us all.

This permeability of boundaries is most strikingly witnessed in the farm itself. The farm is a shelter, a common home to many animals. Houses and barns present a united front to the weather, and their thresholds are crossed all day with no sense that either is more sacrosanct than the other. The human quarters are cleaner and quieter; but they lie under the same jurisdiction, which is one of work and need, not privacy.

Molly and Bill live in an old farmhouse of stone set back from the road. The kitchen was added in the fifties, and its exterior of grey concrete blocks, punctuated by metal-framed windows, clashes with the sandy stonework of the original cottage, giving it a character at once grim, forbidding and temporary.

This kitchen is the most important room in the house. Its door commands a view of the barns and sheep-pens, and has become the main entrance to the farm. Inside is a floor of patterned linoleum and a large Formica table on which food is served. There is a white patch on the discoloured wall where a Georgian sideboard stood, until the *Antiques Roadshow* came on the telly and siphoned the past away. The remaining furniture is sparse and cheap. Two Windsor chairs stand before the fireplace, which is taken up by a cast-iron stove. There are scores of knick-knacks, but none of them were chosen: some were given; most were collected as trophies. Photographs of departed children and prize-winning sows stand side by side, joint proof of Molly's skill at breeding.

As you enter you are aware that you are not crossing a threshold between the public and the private. This is simply the place where the humans are kept, and the containers and implements stand to human needs in the same relation as those in the barn stand to the needs of bovines. On the electric cooker is a heavy frying pan, and beside it a loaf of bread, a jar of fat and a tray of duck eggs, porcelain white in the ambient sunlight. The diet is old-fashioned, but the kitchen is no stage-set for *Cold Comfort Farm*. There are no earthenware milk jugs and no flitches of bacon hooked to the rafters. Molly is a modern person, who buys in the supermarket. The most important item of furniture is the freezer, against which there leans a large sack of potatoes. And above the sink, visible from the table, is the television, which flickers soundlessly, an outpost of the urban glare. This room is the inside of Molly's farm, but it is also an outside, like the breezy barns across the yard. All visitors are entertained here, and in summer the door is never closed.

On very special occasions, however, another room is opened, an inner parlour across the stairwell, part of the original farmhouse, with thick stone walls, and tiny windows that shed a sparse yellow light. The furniture here is Edwardian – a heavy couch, two leather armchairs with velvet cushions and a vast oak dresser burdened with unused china. The air is slightly damp, since the chimney has been blocked by an electric fire. The flower-patterned wallpaper, like the thick red carpet, is new and the only departure from the spick and span orderliness is made by the thunder flies that have crept behind the glass of the sporting prints above the dresser. You might suppose that this room, which is the true inside of Molly's house, is also the rural equivalent of the private space to which urban people come home from their adventures.

The curious thing, however, is that it is not a private space at all. Molly's parlour is, in its way, a yet more public space than Molly's kitchen. For the parlour has a ceremonial function. It is the room where even the most distant stranger can be invited and still remain a stranger. The parlour is opened up for christenings and funerals, or on special birthdays when neighbours come. But it has no personality, and repudiates all thought of self or solitude. It is part of the common habitat, hidden away, to be sure, but not because it has anything to hide. The parlour, like the telly screen, is a space at the periphery of Molly's life, a space where the unknown and the unknowable give their brief greetings, then go on their way.

The permeability of rural boundaries is illustrated in another way by the hunt, which Molly regularly follows on foot. Whether or not you approve of hunting, it is worth considering its role in the building and breaching of boundaries, since this is an indispensable route to the social, historical and cultural meaning of the English landscape and of the forms of human life that have grown in it.

English aristocrats, unlike the French, have always preferred the country to the town, and hunting has always been one of their highest priorities. However, hunting with hounds requires the cooperation of neighbours; and in the countryside neighbours tend to be farmers. Hence hunting has encouraged squire, tenant and farmer to view their locality as a common domain – a tendency that can be witnessed from the earliest Middle Ages, when the yeoman farmer became an accepted and influential part of the landscape.[14] In England the old contest for territory between hunter and farmer gave way to another and more modern conflict, in which farmer and hunter stand together against the intruder from the town.

In England, therefore, we witness the co-existence, as in a puzzle painting, of two visions of the landscape: that of the farmer, fiercely protecting his bounded patch, and that of the hunter, led from place to place by a quarry that recognizes neither boundaries nor laws but only the ubiquitous distinction between safety and danger. On hunting days parcelled-out farmland is suddenly transformed into the common land of the hunter-gatherer, and as suddenly lapses into its husbanded state as the hue and cry recedes. In the poetry of John Clare, in the novels of Fielding and Trollope, and in the paintings of Cotman and Crome we find striking representations of a countryside that is, as it were, doubled up, folded into two rival maps, and bearing the indelible marks of each. Nor is this doubling of the landscape witnessed only in the serious art and literature of rural England. It is equally evident in popular art and decoration. On biscuit boxes, crockery, table mats and wall prints the images of the chase are endlessly reproduced, usually dwelling on those aspects – the meet, the goodnight, the homeward-wending horsemen – that evoke the collective settlement of the land. The country pub establishes its credentials as a 'wayside inn' by decorating its walls with hunting prints; and the most popular song ever composed in England – 'D'ye ken John Peel?', in which the culture of hunting is lovingly surveyed and endorsed – is still sung here, long after the repertoire of folk song has vanished from the rural consciousness.

Plato wrote, in *The Laws*, that: 'there can be no more important kind of information than the exact knowledge of your own
country; and for this as well as for more general reasons of pleasure and advantage, hunting with hounds...should be pursued by
the young.' Plato's sentiments are still alive in England, and help to
explain the peculiar excitements of hunting. The thrill of jumping
is not – as many people imagine – merely an equestrian experience.
It is the thrill that comes from the dissolution of a boundary, and
the annihilation of all the artificial claims of title that go with it.
You do this in intimate conjunction with an animal, in full and
blood-warming empathy with a pack of hounds. For a brief
moment you are laying aside the demands of farming, and the
man-centred individualism that farming engenders, and roaming
across a landscape that is shared. This sense of common ownership
and common destiny is part of what turns the land into a landscape. The fields that we see from our window do not end at our
boundary but stretch beyond it, to the place where the hounds of
the Vale of the White Horse hunt must be called off from the territory of the Old Berkshire, where 'ours' becomes 'theirs', and the
riot of followers must turn at last for home.

This subsumption by the mystical collective is apparent in the
costumes, the ritual gestures and the quasi-liturgical words that
accompany hunting. It is especially apparent in the headgear.
Whether you attend the meet on horseback, on foot or in a car,
some form of hat is obligatory, and this hat must be touched and
doffed with obsessive regularity if you are to justify your presence
in the team. You may think that the hunting cap is worn for safety's sake. In fact it is part of a complex form of social communica-
tion, in which old customs are revisited and old manners revived.

The head is the seat of intelligence, the source of speech, and the
object of our glances. By wearing a hat you place a frame around
your personality, and so cross the threshold from private to public,
engaging with strangers on conventional terms. The wearing of hats
was therefore an important part of our ancestors' attempt to create
a public realm, in which people could be correctly dressed and part
of the furniture. From the sombrero to the city bowler, from the
stovepipe to the tarboosh, the hat was a form of good manners, a
way of recognizing others by putting a lid on the self.

That is why people doffed their hats. The proud sweep of the
three-cornered hat, the humble clasping of the cap against the

chest, the polite raising of the topper: all these were attempts to establish a relationship, while confirming the social order that gave sense to it. And if the social order was disapproved of, so was the hat. Atatürk's law on hats, made immovable by the Turkish constitution, forbids the wearing of the fez, symbol and enforcer of a repudiated past. The bowler hat, once ubiquitous in London, is now unwearable in the city. Judges and lawyers are trying to escape their wigs, and mortar-boards have all but gone from our universities.

To remove your hat was to step out of the public and protected realm, to make yourself both physically and personally vulnerable, and to prepare yourself for private things. Hence the need to bare your head when entering a room or when addressing another. Hence the insolence of a cocked hat – half on, half off, revealing that the other's presence is of no concern to you. Hats were words in a complex language, and learning their grammar was a part of growing up.

This ancient grammar is what we witness in the hunting field. The top hat is still officially correct, and the hunting cap is tolerated only by a frail convention that might be rescinded at any time. Moreover, the cap should be secured by its rim alone, so that it can be lifted, doffed and extended as the etiquette requires. This etiquette embraces the foot-followers, whose cloth caps are raised and flourished as frequently as the caps of the riders. To the visiting anthropologist, a meet of foxhounds is one of the most remarkable visions of our country, since it shows a language as dead as Latin being used with all the expressiveness of poetry – rather as Latin was handled in the medieval schools. And of course this is one source of the hostility to hunting. Uniforms are exclusive. And the language of hats is like the foreign tongue that confirms the strangeness and inhumanity of the invading tribe.

The tribal aspect of hunting is most apparent when the hunt meets on your farm. The event begins the day before, with a visit from the master. Our master is a farmer, born and bred here. He has known the residents for three generations, and speaks in his broad Wiltshire accent with intimate understanding of the fields and coverts, as though he himself had charge of them. He tells you where he wants to go and his voice quavers with emotion, as though describing a favourite child. His role is like that of the shaman, mystically summoning the souls that live in fields and trees. And for a day thereafter you live in this transfigured territory, in which every tree and hedgerow, every ditch and gate, looks back at you with the face of collective ownership.

It is half-past ten when the tribe begins its invasion. They come in battered cars, on bicycles, on horseback. Every trade is represented, from roofer to ratter and from farrier to vet. The distinction between the mounted followers and the rest is not one of class or wealth: the local plumber comes on horseback; the local landowner stumbles from field to field in her boots.

First to arrive is the band of retired farm-hands, led by Percy, who seems to have only two teeth – one upper incisor and one lower – and who carries in his arms a one-eyed terrier with the same ratty grin as its master. From time to time Percy will take a mouth organ from his pocket and give an expert medley of Scottish reels. He shouts in mock anger at each new arrival and then, softening his tone, enquires about the sheep, the wife or the tractor, secure in the shared attitudes that such subjects invoke. Some of those who appear are thatchers, hedgers or coppicers from the time when those trades were viable. During their youth and manhood these old tradesmen plied between the farms on Bantam motorbikes, since cars were unaffordable luxuries. And when they were too old to balance on their bikes, they acquired three-wheelers, which can be driven with a motorcycle licence. I look inside one of these curious vehicles: an old Robin Reliant parked on our verge. It contains a thermos, a sandwich box, a spade, a bill-hook, and a pair of rubber boots. It is not a holiday vehicle but a day-to-day companion, designed to visit familiar places, where the driver is greeted by the things, the people and the animals that he knows.

Some of the women wear tough country clothes, with wellies under woollen skirts. The younger ones have children in tow, and Rosalind leads her three-year-old daughter on a Shetland pony. The yard rapidly fills with people, and the verges with cars. At twenty to eleven the hunt box arrives, bringing the huntsman, the whipper-in, the kennel groom, the horses and the hounds. It stands in the centre of the yard, mesmerizing people and animals with the hidden life that whines and whickers inside. The horses are now pirouetting in their stables and kicking the doors; conversation is warm and general, and the huntsman, descending slowly from the horsebox in his brilliant uniform, walks like a monarch through the sea of greetings.

Of course, we expected to give breakfast to the huntsman. What we had not expected was a retinue like Lear's knights – kennel hands, whippers-in, terrier-men, farmers, rat-catchers, masters, ex-masters, and old boys for whom there is no explanation except that they have been around too long to need one – all stamping across the threshold in search of whisky, sausages and tea. Conversation touches every relevant subject from heiffers to hedges and from scenting to setts. Only one topic is conspicuously avoided, and that is the Government's hostility to hunting. For these people the end of their way of life is unacceptable, and the thought of it is hazy and wordless like the thought of death.

After 20 minutes, when the house is swollen with their talk and no longer ours, they go out into the yard.The tailboard of the box comes down, the hounds rush out into the sea of legs, and the horses come stamping down the ramp like angry troopers. The resemblance between the 100 gathered faces is not so much a matter of culture or breeding, as of life and landscape. One woman in scruffy slacks of wool and worsted owns 1000 acres; another squats in a pony paddock down the road. But their faces shine with the same attachment to the place and the life that they are here to celebrate. The master gives a speech of thanks, and it is as though our membership has at last been recognized – but only on the understanding that the farm is common property and we its temporary trustees.

There is a short toot on the horn, and the pack assembles around the hunstman's horse, moving like a fluttering skirt towards the hillside. The band of horses, bicycles, cars and people moves like an exultant caravan across its collective territory, enjoying as a common possession what tomorrow will once again be parcelled into lots. And at the end of the day, when the huntsman and his 20 knights come clattering and mud-encrusted into our living room, loud, anecdotal and elated, we yield immediately, since the house, like the landscape, is theirs. We have been granted a glimpse of another world, a world that we share with the animals, who are dignified as antagonists, worshipped as totems and pursued as quarry. You may welcome this or you may deplore it; but that is what hunting means.

Among those who deplore it none has had more impact on rural life than the RSPCA. The society was founded in the early nineteenth century, with the support of hunting people and largely as a protest against the way horses and dogs were treated in cities. It is now controlled by cat-lovers, few of whom have much understanding of wildlife or any real desire to conserve it. Shortly after the hunt met at our house a circular came from the RSPCA, telling all members to write to the Prime Minister supporting his policy to ban hunting with dogs. We were mildly astonished to discover that the animal illustrated as the beneficiary of this initiative was not a bright little fox-cub, but a mink, its lethal incisors bared, and its close-set evil eyes clearly focused on some enemy – presumably one of those sanctimonious RSPCA inspectors who make even gentle old ladies bare their fangs.

The circular told us that the use of dogs to hunt mink is unacceptable, and recommended instead that the animals be caught in traps, and subsequently despatched (presumably after a day or so of leisurely retirement behind bars) by a humane killer. The previous year, however, the RSPCA had campaigned for a total ban on the fur trade, arguing that it is intolerable to mink to be kept behind bars. Putting the two campaigns together I realized that the RSPCA – or at least its campaigning arm – doesn't in fact care about mink at all. It has merely conceived a hatred, first for those who wear fur, second for followers of hounds (mink-hounds included).

The RSPCA is in fact two institutions. One has inherited the spirit of the Victorian zoophiles who founded it, the other has inherited their money. The one loves animals, the other hates people. The distinction between them was brought home to our neighbours during the crisis over the live export of calves. While the central office of the RSPCA joined in the national hysteria, our local branch hit on the reasonable solution – which is not to export the calves but to eat them. The inspiration for this policy was Mary, a farming member of the local committee.

After shooting her second calf, Mary decided that she could not do it again. It smacked of impiety, to deliver a young animal from its mother after long and painful hours, and then promptly to kill it. The answer, she concluded, is veal. But here is the dilemma: to enter the continental veal market you must produce meat that is snow-white and anaemic. This means preventing the calves from eating anything except milk, and in particular preventing them from eating straw or other vegetable matter. That is why, on the continent, calves are imprisoned in crates and kept on concrete, a cruel fate for any cloven-footed animal. Fortunately these practices are illegal in England. The consequence, however, is that if the English won't eat Mary's veal, nobody will.

People who have no experience of farming often find it difficult to believe that farmers care for the animals that they breed for meat. If they really cared for them how could they kill them? To think in this way is to confuse two distinct relations – that between a person and a pet, which is a relation of luxury, and that between a farmer and his domestic animals, which is a relation of need. Since breaking into the veal trade Mary's affection for her herd has increased: for the cows are now useful to her, part of a cycle of mutual benefit that gives Mary an added interest in their welfare. The pleasure she feels on letting the Hereford milch cow into the barn, when the calves run to suckle at the udder, is as much a joy in young life as the pleasure of a child playing with a puppy. Mary's calves represent a positive addition to the sum of animal welfare, achieved in defiance of those who stand up for the rights of animals, and who would like to abolish dairy farming – and therefore cows – altogether.

Being a rural member of the RSPCA means caring not merely for animals but for their keepers too. No-one in our community was better at this than Hilda, whose presence among us was that of an elder sister, who filled her days with charitable deeds, who comforted the afflicted and who was not averse to afflicting the comfortable when they did not give as they should. Although Hilda was in many ways a naive person, who accepted the anti-farming propaganda of the RSPCA's central office at face value, she never allowed her prejudices to overcome her compassion. She looked with an equal sympathy on the famished mare and the lonely old farmer who had tethered her, and she tried to help them both. Her first thought was for others, and she enjoyed nothing so much as sharing troubles and studying how to lighten them. Her talents in this matter were so well-known that the American penitentiary service would give her telephone number to prisoners on Death Row, knowing that they would come away from a half-hour talk with Hilda convinced that somebody cared for them and that life had not been in vain.

For some people charitable work is a kind of morbid flight from reality, an obsession with weakness that reveals a poverty of soul. Not so for Hilda. In everything she did she conveyed a warm love of life, an almost festive sense of occasion, and a gladness to be where she was. She came to RSPCA meetings dressed as for an outing, her hair carefully concocted, her ears adorned with clip-on ornaments, her jacket studded with brooches and a clean white kerchief around her neck. Her conversation was full of jokes, but she abhorred gossip, especially hurtful gossip; her gaiety therefore had an air of seriousness, like the gaiety of a priest or a nun. Not that she was puritanical: when the meetings adjourned she was the first to propose a visit to the pub and, were it not for her illness, the signs of which she could conceal only for shortish periods, she would have gladly stayed to the early hours carousing.

Hilda died of cancer, but she also lived from it. It sounds odd to put it that way, but it is the only form of words that I can think of to capture the particular way that she had of incorporating her illness into her life. For Hilda cancer was a means to understand our human lot, and a call to forgiveness. She saw her illness as a gift – the proof that joy is always possible if the heart is not starved. In a certain measure it was the true source of her happiness, and because she accepted it others did the same, and looked on her as whole and warm and normal.

This habit of treating bad luck as the other side of good has not yet disappeared from the farms. Hilda's self-deprecating attitude to misfortune can be observed all over our valley, even among those who have inherited the curmudgeonly spirit of its soil. One reason for this is that farmers are self-employed, and therefore unable to shift their responsibilities onto other shoulders. There was a time when employers and employees were bound only by the contractual relation between them, and when the responsibilities of the employer ceased when the work wasn't done. The employment relation in law is now as complex as that of husband and wife, fraught with rights and duties that have no contractual base. An employee has extensive claims against his employer, even when (especially when) the work isn't done – claims to sick leave, to reparations for unfair dismissal, to maternity leave and even paternity leave.

It is therefore now unwise to employ people if you can avoid it, and certainly unwise to employ them in the official, tax-paying economy which holds you eternally liable for their well-being. This is one reason for the decline in rural employment. Less people are employed on the land, per head of population, in Britain than in

any other country of the world save Singapore, where there is virtually no land in any case – less people even than in Hong Kong!
The work exists in abundance, but no farmer can take the risk of
employing others to perform it, unless they are members of his
immediate family who don't show up on the books, and who can
be relied upon not to claim their exorbitant legal privileges.

The distinction between the employed and the self-employed
creates the only real class division in modern societies, and, like
every class division, it has both an economic and a cultural side.
Farmers organize their lives according to an ethic of self-sufficiency.
They are allowed to grumble, but never to opt out. Two years ago
a gust of influenza laid low half the workforce in Swindon. It
afflicted our neighbours just as severely. But not one of them
ceased to work. Stephen stopped his tractor one afternoon to
inform us in astonished tones that his father had actually gone
upstairs to lie down, the first time in 30 years, so bad did he feel.
And he made it clear that he both pitied his father and resented
him, since Stephen now had to do the milking by himself.

What is true of illnesses is true also of accidents and disabili-
ties, the cost of which on the farm must be borne entirely by the
victim. Last year Tom was hitching a trailer to his tractor when it
rolled back and slammed onto his foot, breaking some bones. In
the compensation culture Tom would have been entitled to several
months of sick leave on full pay, as well as a large handout and
maybe a permanent disability pension too. As it is, he hobbled
around for two months in a plaster, while the neighbours helped
him to keep on top of his farming.

Tom's accident was a proof of his underlying happiness. His
loss was made good not by money extorted from people who were
in no way to blame, but by kind deeds and neighbourly goodwill.
In the culture of compensation these commodites are rapidly disappearing, so leaving us bereft of the things that make our lives
worthwhile. This, however, is what keeps people farming – the
knowledge that the self-sufficiency of the farmer is not only a
virtue in itself, but the passport to rewards that cannot be measured by money.

'He's a bit troublesome that way,' Tom said of his trailer, by
way of coming to terms with the accident. It was as though he had
fallen out with a close companion, and was biding his time till they
could make it up. This way of referring to things as though they

had souls is also part of the ethic of self-sufficiency. If you are not shifting the burden of your life on to anybody else, but bearing it yourself, then problems, tasks, machines and objects seem self-sufficient too, with a mind and a will of their own. They are not the passive levers of the great hand-out machine, but fellow travellers on the wheel of fortune, who have their ups and downs as you do. You confront objects face to face, and this is the true cure for that state which the philosophers describe as alienation – the state in which people see themselves as things – namely, to see things as people.

Ruskin and Morris opposed the piecemeal labour of the urban factories to the trades and crafts that still flourished in the countryside. Unlike Hegel or Marx, they had no theory of alienation; but they believed that the soul is jeopardized by the machine-like tasks that were now required of the body. And for a while their favoured remedy – the restoration of a craft economy – was both attractive and believable. Nevertheless, the crafts took their inexorable way to extinction. Basket-weaving, for example, is as necessary a craft today as it was at the time of William Morris, when our farmers in the claylands laid out osier-beds and withy-aits, and when they grew willow for coppicing, some kinds esteemed for their elasticity, others for their durability or strength. They knew 80 varieties of willow, many dependent for their properties on the soil and climate where they grew: the Berkshire long-bud, for example, the black maul of Northants, the Welsh grey with green tops, and the whip-lash withy from the sedgemour rhines. But baskets are now imported and the willow coppices have declined to scrubland.

Many other features of the landscape and its buildings speak in similar ways of vanished crafts. Roofs remind us of thatchers, who also sewed up the hay-ricks and proofed them against the rain. External walls bear the mark of stone masons, internal walls that of the pargeters who embossed the plaster with their moulds; waggons (still rotting in our local barns) bring joiners and wheelwrights to mind. All the subsidiary trades of the farm had their single-minded experts whose lives were built around their work, and who brought to that work the love of detail which is one half of living in a settled way.

Each town had its cobbler, saddler, farrier, glassmaker, glover, and cabinet-maker; and the work of the farm was parcelled out between the shepherd, the drover, the ploughboy, the swineherd and the reaper. Peculiar trades are mentioned in the literature of Victorian England: the 'drowner' who controlled the water meadows, the 'reddleman' (described in *The Return of the Native*), or – my own favourite – the 'crow-starver'. Many of these trades sound so quaintly on the tongue that the casual observer might suppose that now nothing is left of the craft economy besides the romantic dreams of Ruskin and Morris.

Soon after my arrival here I entered Molly's open kitchen and caught sight of a darning last – that peculiar mushroom-shaped object which bridges the holes in socks as they are mended. It stood upside down on the mantelpiece, at just the place where my mother had kept hers. Soon I came to understand that the habit of repairing things can never be dispensed with if you live on a farm. Farmers, like sailors, spend half their day repairing things, and, like sailors, they have a life-and-death relation with the things that they mend. Each year requires you to heal the wounds of the last one, mending fences, hanging gates, stitching rugs, welding machinery, clearing drains and ditches, adapting sheds to new uses, and repairing the pipework in the fields. In all those ways a kind of craft economy endures on the farm, and spreads its influence around itself, leading even the incomers to adopt the habit of mending what they might otherwise carelessly throw away.

And there are still crafts that engage the whole life of those who practice them. These too are endorsed by the incomers. Take the cobbler, for instance, hero of countless fairy tales, and exalted into the epitome of wisdom and public spirit in *Die Meistersinger von Nürnberg*. Shoes are shaped by our use of them, become friendlier with the years, and are never seen as quite replaceable. We experience the earth through the medium they provide, so that they become a part of us. We are therefore prepared to subsidize cobblers, long after it has become cheaper to regard our shoes as 'disposable'.

Our cobbler in Malmesbury is a lover of shoes, who perfectly exemplifies what Ruskin and Morris were trying, in their arch and moralizing way, to get across to their contemporaries. Mustafa sees the soul in the sole, and the wearer in the worn. Shoes, for him, are the middle terms in human relations, objects of respect, and signs of his own social value. He takes them from you with an intent preoccupied smile, examines them, and then lovingly describes first their defects, then the very great virtues, apparent to his expert eye, which justify the cost of mending them. And because he can live from his skills, and at the same time express himself through them, Mustafa is a happy person, who is as comfortable in an English farming community as he was in his Turkish village.

There is another shoe-craft on which our rural economy entirely depends, which is that of the farrier. Horse shoes must be fitted exactly, not to the hoofs only, but to a horse's way of moving, to his way of growing, and to his temperament. The knowledge required of a farrier is so great and intricate that three years of apprenticeship are required of those who enter the profession. Furthermore the Worshipful Company of Farriers keeps vigilant watch over standards, and confers fellowships on those who show true practical skill.

Andrew, our farrier, is a Fellow of the Worshipful Company. His apprentices learn from him more than a craft. They learn a way of life, a habit of dedication, and an ability to defer to the one who really knows. This habit of deference towards knowledge is the real way to acquire it, and it is more often to be observed in apprentices than scholars. Watching Andrew's way of teaching, I have come to the conclusion that there is no such thing as a useless craft or a supplanted skill. If you learn your skills in the right way, by deferring to the one who already possesses them, and giving your whole self to their exercise, then you fit yourself for the acquisition of any other skill you might need. Skills properly learned are by their nature transferable. This means that the rural economy is a vast, unexploited and largely unexplored source of human capital.

Self-employed people like Andrew, Mustafa, and so many others who live in our place, ought to be set before us as examples not only of the 'unalienated labour' of which socialists have always dreamed, but also of the 'responsible free enterprise' esteemed by the defenders of capitalism. In the case of farmers, however, both these aspects of their work are obscured by policy and rendered imperceivable by subsidies. In the eyes of our government, the English farmer is someone who has been far too kindly treated for far too long, and who needs now to confront realities. This was brought home to me by Sidney, upon whom we all depend for our morale, whose smiling countenance brightens our local meetings, who has suffered every hardship cheerfully, who has seen his debts and his workload mounting in tandem, whose old farm dwindles with his purse but who nevertheless thanks the Lord that he was born and bred a farmer. Sidney burst into my office one day waving a copy of the *Telegraph*, and crying 'That's it, I'm finished, it's all over!'

He had experimented with these words before, but always with a shy and tentative expression, quickly conquered by a smile. This time it is serious, and he slaps the paper down on my desk like a death warrant, jabbing his thick finger at the article that has chilled his bones. It tells us that Lord Haskins, Chairman of Northern Foods, head of the Government's Better Regulation Task Force and Grand Panjandrum of the Food Standards Agency is to launch a semi-official Inquiry into the future of European Rural Society. His lordship, by way of proving his eminent suitability for this new task, has announced that 'farmers have been mollycoddled for too long', and that we should cut their numbers by half. No subsidies, bigger farms, redundancy payments to farmers and environmental support schemes – such, in brief, is the Haskins remedy for the present crisis, and as for the old rural idyll, that was nothing better than a myth. The nineteenth-century farmer, he tells us, was hungry and poverty-stricken, and his one ambition was 'to get the hell out of the countryside'.

Well, Sidney, I say, these are the opinions of an expert, and one close to the heart of our rulers. Who are we to protest? And in any case, what do you object to? Subsidies have all gone to the big boys, to the absentee landlords, to the corn barons and their shareholders. And by forcing up the price of land, they have driven the small family farmer like yourself out of business.

'Of course, I know all that,' he replies. 'It's the tone I object to. Who does this man think he is, to describe people who work a twelve-hour day seven days a week, for an average income of ten thousand a year, who have now seen their animals slaughtered for no real reason and their way of life destroyed, who is this man to describe us as mollycoddled? And who is doing the mollycoddling, I ask you? Not Northern Foods, which drives the same hard bargain as Sainsbury's or Tesco's.'

I agree, 'mollycoddled' is not a very sensitive choice of words. But wake up: this is the postmodern world. 'Sensitivity' is for single mothers, ethnic minorities, asylum seekers – definitely not for people so redolent of old England as *farmers*. Now, in France...

'Yes, I know. In France someone like Lord Haskins would be well supplied with manure. But the fight's gone out of me.'

Sidney is silent for a moment.

'I'll tell you what though,' he resumes. 'There's more to this than meets the eye. Us farmers have been battling with the supermarkets from the moment they came on the scene. And everything that has been bad for us has been good for them. Paperwork, for example, which only they can cope with, food safety standards, which the big distributor can use to close down the local competition and keep us in chains. Yes, and subsidies, which mean the land is owned by the same boys as own the supermarkets. And who is this man as is now in charge of all these things? A supermarket boss.'

But this is the post-democratic world, Sidney. There is a new and improved way of doing things. Experts are now self-appointed, peerages are given to cronies, elected officers are replaced by commissars, and decisions are made by those with the greatest interest in the outcome: how else can we guarantee change? Or are we to muddle along in the old way, appointing impartial judges, allowing functionless people like you and me to have a say in things, and so preventing anything from happening?

'And this stuff about the starving farmers,' Sidney continues, ignoring me. 'My ancestors farmed here in the nineteenth century: I still have their account books. They did very well, I can tell you. As did their neighbours. They loved the land, just like I do.'

But Sidney, you cannot expect a busy man like Lord Haskins to read irrelevant authors like Thomas Hardy or George Eliot, and in any case the past has been remodelled on socialist principles. Maybe it wasn't true *then* that they were starving; but it is definitely true *now* – you can see it on TV.

Sidney looks at me for a moment, and at last begins to smile.

'So you mean the whole thing's a fiction?'

Neither fiction nor fact, I answer. Lord Haskins owes his fortune to one of the most environmentally destructive and most subsidized businesses in the modern economy – a business obscenely mollycoddled even before its chieftains were recruited, like Lords Haskins and Sainsbury, to govern us. He has no qualifications that fit him (in your eyes or mine) for the positions that he occupies. Still less is he qualified to pontificate about the countryside. He is a Party apparatchik, charged with concealing the truth about rural Britain. And the truth, Sidney, is you.

To say as much is not to deny that Sidney has benefited from subsidies and planning exemptions; nor is it to give way to the

fantasy of a new agrarian future, in which food will be locally produced and locally consumed, by organic methods that leave the
soil unaltered. It is to recognize that the principal product of the
soil is not crops but people. Changes in farming lead to changes in
the farmer. Those celebrated lines of Goldsmith's ring as true today
as when he wrote them, observing his childhood village from
which the population had fled:

> Princes and lords may flourish, or may fade;
> A breath can take them, as a breath has made;
> But a bold peasantry, their country's pride,
> When once destroyed can never be supplied.

Sidney is not a peasant but a yeoman farmer, whose ancestors
of many generations lie buried in Somerford churchyard. But he
exemplifies the peasant virtues extolled by Goldsmith, and those
virtues are to my way of thinking as necessary now as they ever
were. Many of the skills that Sidney possesses are shared by people
who are not farmers. But only in the farmer are they synthesized into
a nugget of human competence which is also a one-ness with the
world of things. Farming skills are acquired through companionship: working side by side in those silent but cheerful moments that
vindicate what Unamuno called the tragic sense of life. That is
why they are handed down in families, rather than taught in
schools. Environmentalists urge us to take up virtual farming,
carefully preserving the veneer of a landscape that was shaped by
productive labour. Real farming is not about the veneer but about
the underlying essence, which is profit. Take away the profit and
the veneer, which was only a by-product and never a goal, will
disintegrate. And no urban incomer, however motivated, will be
able to put it back again.

People have been lamenting the flight from the countryside
since Virgil's *Georgics*; and William Cobbett, in his *Rural Rides*,
was as grimly negative about the matter as H. J. Massingham in his
famous articles in *The Field*. A century and a half separates those
last two writers, and yet the one great fact remains – namely, that
young people do not stay on the farms. Far from being a new and
lamentable development, this fact is a permanent feature of
Western civilization. Moreover, it is the explanation of much that
we love in city life, and much that we love in the country.

English primogeniture ensured that, of those born on the land, only the oldest would inherit. Younger sons, obliged to look elsewhere for a livelihood, migrated to the towns in search of a trade. Meanwhile the farm remained intact, a symbol of home and its unchanging rhythms. The young people who left the farm retained memories of its tranquillity and sweetness. They cultivated this image in their quiet moments, and looked from the windows of their urban lodgings on to an imagined landscape of their childhood. This imaginary England was later immortalized in literature and art, by people who knew it only from the deep unconscious residue of feeling that their ancestors once brought from the farm. The *Wind-in-the-Willows* vision of our countryside, which is the main spiritual resource of the English when they find themselves in trouble far from home, is due to the fact that most English people now live in towns.

We should not think that life in the country, for those young people who remain there, is dull. The children of farmers invariably have hobbies. Young Harry, our neighbour, is an aficionado of caged birds, which he trades with fellow enthusiasts all over the district. Harry takes only one day off each year, in order to go with his father to the agricultural show at Moreton-in-Marsh, there to exchange hints, tips, anecdotes and goodwill with others for whom this is likewise their day of renewal. All the hardship feeds into this festive day, and is also redeemed by it. Rare breeds and unusual exhibits send Harry back home in a meditative frame of mind, and every now and then he toys with the idea of diversifying into llamas, alpacas or ostriches. But always he rejects the tempting novelties, and re-applies himself to his sheep and cows. For that was his father's way and his father's father's before him, and the challenge is to keep things going. This holding fast to custom is the root idea of primogeniture, and one reason why our countryside has retained so much of its beauty.

Undeniably, however, the isolation of the family farm makes for difficulties when it comes to sex. The nearest pubs are accessible to our neighbours only by car, and to drive there is to risk your licence. Trips to London, or even to Bath and Bristol, are virtually ruled out by the long working hours required of the younger generation. And if they want to dance our farmers' children must normally make the trip to Swindon, to go clubbing in the Brunel Rooms, owned and run by Bill, our former Master of Foxhounds.

Unless, that is, someone has organized a barn dance in the neighbourhood. The spontaneous dances of rustic people have not, on
the whole, won the approval of moralizing painters like Brueghel.
But they have charmed the great composers. From Bach to Bartók,
rustic dance steps have provided the core of rhythmical organiza-
tion, and when Chopin and Smetana turned their attention to the
syncopated dances of Slavonic peasants they changed the course of
modern music. Folk song and folk dance were thenceforth to be a
leading source of musical inspiration, the image in music of the
human community at peace.

'The dancers are all gone under the hill', wrote Eliot: but what
about Eliot – was he under the hill or over the top? Certainly,
young people brought up in modern cities don't learn much about
the old kind of dancing. Steps, formations, changes, even partners
are not really necessary to the disco floor, since the music annihi-
lates social gestures. Disco dancing is not a social discipline, but
an individual release. Hence older people cannot join in, and sex
occupies the foreground. The idea of dancing as a ceremony, in
which courtesy and deference are the guiding principles, is not
merely unfamiliar to most young people, but apt to appear ridicu-
lous in their eyes.

In our part of the world, however, thanks to its relative isolation and the enduring need to overcome it, the barn dance still
exists. Admittedly, it is not a very sophisticated affair and only a
few old hands like Sidney and Margaret really know how to set it
up. Nevertheless, for all their quaintness, our barn dances are real
social occasions, not remotely like the communist folk festivals
satirized by Malcolm Bradbury in his portrait of Slaka. The barn
dance is a way of coming to terms with the fact that, in rural areas,
there are not enough young people to reach the critical mass
required for dancing. Whenever a barn dance is announced, to
raise funds for charity, or to celebrate a birthday, people of all ages
come from surrounding farms and stand in their lines, men on one
side, women opposite, and prepare to renew their tenacious sense
of neighbourhood.

The music is provided by a band of accordion, violin and bass,
sometimes helped out by an electronic keyboard or a rhythm
machine, and 'talked through' by an impresario with a deafening
microphone. The dances are crude. Nothing is required by way of
steps except the shuffle and skip of the walk-on Shakespearean

shepherd. The tunes are muddled and the patterns simple. But still, there is a naïve exuberance in the event, and a strengthening of the bond between old and young. Line dances were originally a kind of intelligence test, an ordeal that the villagers might pass or fail, and an opportunity for the young to make themselves attractive. In the days before sexual intercourse, such dances provided young lovers with the means to amplify, and also to conceal, their mutual attraction, and to sow, in the midst of the social ritual, the subversive seeds of desire. At the same time, they renewed the experience of community as a collective adventure, with a past and future that out-ran the course of love. That, briefly, is why these dances existed, and why they have lost so little of their appeal.

Barn dances are not the only social dances in our community. Each year around Burns' Night an evening of Scottish reels takes place, in the vast Italianate mansion of Westonbirt, built 130 years ago by Robert Holford, and now a school for girls. The evening is organized by young people from the surrounding villages, who prepare the food, serve from the bar and do their best to put the oldies at their ease. It is not so difficult to mix young and old, pretty and plain, when all are wearing formal clothes. The long dresses act like those rococo frames in the art museum, which draw attention to the pictures, and also away from them, so enabling a mediocre Greuze to share the wall-space with a sublime Leonardo.

Scottish country dancing is not by origin a rural institution. The word 'country' comes from French *contré*, meaning face to face, and the dances originated in the French and Scottish courts. Nevertheless, it is only in rural conditions that you can really get into the spirit of them. For it is only in those conditions that old and young still share their pleasures. Many of the younger people have just about mastered the *pas de Basque*, and haven't a clue where to turn or with whom. Others have taken secret or not-so-secret lessons. Others still have an astonishing repertoire of steps and gestures, and are able to shout instructions as they swing themselves from one dancing pillar to the next, like monkeys leaping from bough to bough in a human forest.

But the most agreeable sight is that of the older generation, many of them stiff at the joints and fighting their twinges, but dancing lightly and serenely, with subdued and reminiscing smiles. The young girls in their swirling dresses are no more interesting than the porcelain dowagers, as they bob and bounce like dolls down the ranks of partners. These old ladies are not reliving their youth, but raising youth and age to a common height of jubilation. Formation dances banish the sexual motive to the background, and allow elegance and vitality to claim their due, regardless of years. They are part of the great work of civilization, which veneers the human animal with a person's face.

Formal dancing also helps you to be reconciled to the human lot. Walk out into the frosty night, so as to listen to the sound from a distance, and you can hear the dance slipping away from you into the past. As it fades into the background, it joins the other dances that have happened on this spot of earth. Youth, sex and life evaporate, until the ghosts all move together in a dream. You understand then that these moments of intense and purposeless community are the reason why we exist.

3

Our Animals

Nothing pleases me more on my morning rides than the view of Farmer Vincent's herd on the hill next to ours. Formed over many decades, with no respect for breed or style or pedigree, it contains black and white Friesians, golden Jerseys, Belgian Blues, sandy Charolets, grey, dun, nutmeg, brindled and liver-coloured mongrels, and a remarkable old matron who is white on one side and terra cotta on the other. It is fortunate that Mr Vincent's cows showed no sign of BSE; for he would never have recovered from the loss of them. Not that Mr Vincent could make any money by selling his herd: its value is not pecuniary but historical and aesthetic – like the value of a gnarled oak tree, or a clump of willows by a pond. Mr Vincent's herd is part of the landscape, and as important to the visible order as the hedgerows that stitch the fields.

There are not many places in the world where you can still see cattle ruminating in pasture. All over France and Germany there are beef cattle and dairy cows: but most of them are locked away, even in summer. Here and there in Poland you will see solitary Friesians in the meadows: look closely, however, and you will discover the iron chains that tether them, and the scorched circles where they have grazed. Cuyp's langorous heifers have largely disappeared from the Dutch landscape (or what is left of it), and the herds that lounge in the ranches of Spain are mostly *toros,* enjoying those years of luxury before their 15 minutes of fame. In England, however, cows are so much part of the scenery that we hardly notice them, until the moment in November when they are no longer there.

Like the landscape, the cow is a man-made object. This helpless box-shaped imbecile on tottering legs, with bloated udders and

61

toothless mouth, was bred for human uses, and steadily deprived
of the ability to survive on her own. Yet the cow is also an animal,
as remote from us in her feelings as any creature of the wild. Living
and working with cows you are immersed in the natural order,
responding not to reason or emotion but to instinct and need. The
cow is the channel through which nature feeds us – literally, by
giving us milk, and also morally, by putting us side by side with
silent herds in a living landscape.

When people describe what they love in the English countryside, they mention the many small green fields with their meticulous boundaries; the streams that run through pasture, and the
copses that crown the hills; sometimes too they remember the
shady trees in the parklands, their branches cropped level six feet
above the ground. These features of the landscape were made
either by cows or for them. Every children's animal book dwells on
the cow as the moral centre of the farmyard. Not for nothing does
the Koran open with the great Surah of the Cow, describing the
reluctant sacrifice of a perfect animal at the command of Moses.
Not for nothing do the Hindus venerate this creature, who so perfectly illustrates the interdependence of nature and man.

During the war my family was billeted on a farm in the village
of Buslingthorpe, Lincolnshire, and the farmer's wife, who became
our Auntie Addie, supplied my mother with the milk she needed for
her children. Auntie Addie's situation as a small-scale producer of
milk and meat was not comfortable, but it was stable. The situation of the dairy farmer had been settled in 1933 by the formation
of the Milk Marketing Board. This was a statutory cooperative
which guaranteed the profits of the dairy farmer in the face of
manipulative strategies by the big dairy companies, while guaran-
teeing a constant and reliable supply of milk for the British people.

The arrangement proved to be one small but significant part of
the war effort, since it had encouraged farmers to keep their dairy
herds and to continue applying themselves to one of the hardest
and most relentless forms of agricultural production, in the face of
fierce competition from abroad. In consequence the British people
were supplied throughout the war with milk, cheese and butter –
not as well supplied as the Scrutons were by Auntie Addie, but well
enough to survive their greatest trial. The Milk Marketing Board
set up its own ancillary dairy company, Dairy Crest, in order to
process the excess product that could not sell at the regulated

price. Between them the two companies stabilized the production and marketing of milk in Britain, and offered one of the few successful examples of price regulation in a free economy.

Partly as a result of the war, milk became a mark of national self-sufficiency, and the dairy herd a symbol of the countryside and its nurturing powers. Successive governments were aware of the precariousness of a business which, despite producing one of the most valuable of all human foodstuffs, could at any moment collapse under the pressure of competition from foreign producers less scrupulous in their treatment of their animals than the British dairy farmer. Hence the Milk Marketing Board was kept in place. Local councils encouraged dairy farming, and three of the farms along our road were built after the war by the County Council, in order to maintain the level of milk production. This is one reason why English pastures survived – for they would not have survived, had they not been re-settled by dairy farmers. The functionalist council houses in which our neighbours live are the price we pay for the landscape.

In 1994, in its urge to prove that it could de-regulate *something* at least, the lame government of John Major picked on the most vulnerable and the most indispensable section of the national economy, and abolished the Milk Marketing Board. It also forbade farmers to retain more than a 50 per cent share in Dairy Crest. To protect the small producers a voluntary cooperative – Milk Marque – was established. The dairies saw their advantage; they first bid up the price of milk, so attracting the farmers away from Milk Marque, and then began to force it down, to the point where they are now offering less than the cost of production. Milk Marque has now been dissolved, following an amazing report from the Monopolies and Mergers Commission which, instead of blaming the commercial dairies for their cartel-like dealings, has blamed the only institution which has tried to give a voice to British dairy farmers. Meanwhile the NFU takes the side of whatever establishment might offer knighthoods and peerages to its leaders, the Government confers honours and even offices on the heads of supermarkets, and the farmers are left, as ever, with no-one to represent them but themselves.

Our neighbours have come to recognize, therefore, what French farmers have always known: that direct action is their only recourse. And if anything were to demonstrate the fundamental decency and patriotism of British farmers, it is the kind of direct action that they resort to. No blocking of roads, burning of crops, releasing of sheep or assaulting of lorry drivers, but merely a nocturnal attendance at the supermarket depot, in order to prevent the lorries from leaving until an audience has been granted. Our local farmers, whose haggard faces by day reveal their stress, appear in the sour yellow light of the 'distribution park' with expressions of hope and resolution. The police, the security guards, even the lorry drivers whose routine they disturb are in sympathy with them; surely, then, someone 'up there' will notice when they raise their voice. And indeed, the supermarkets have begun to meet the men who picket their depots, and to appoint officers to note down their grievances. But who will listen to those officers, when they file their reports? And who, in a Parliament where the supermarkets have so powerful a voice, both inside and outside government, will listen to people who can survive only at a cost to the supermarkets? Our farmers are crying over spilt milk; but maybe they are crying to the people who milk them.

Such are the follies we have had to live through in our neighbourhood and the wonder is that the cows are still there – unprofitable as Mr Vincent's, but clung to as a kind of moral necessity, proof of our collective will to survive.

What is it, exactly, that binds a farmer to his herd? The question can be asked of every farmyard animal, and has a single answer, namely respect: not the respect of man for animal, but that of animal for man. Xenophanes of Colophon, who lived in the sixth century BC, ridiculed the anthropomorphic deities of his fellow Greeks. If oxen, horses and lions had hands with which to paint, he wrote, then they too would make images of gods. And the gods of oxen would look like oxen, those of horses would resemble horses, and those of lions would be lions.

Any farmer will tell you how wrong Xenophanes was. Domestic animals already have gods, and the shape of these gods is human.

Two dozen cows are standing on straw in our cow-shed, their heads deep in silage, their digestive systems contentedly at work. From morn to night they stare quietly into the middle distance, immersed in the oceanic consciousness of herds. They view each other as natural features of the environment, and except when a calf is taken from its mother, they feel neither grief at the departure of an old companion, nor joy at the arrival of a new one. Their worldview is placid, undemanding and incurious. Only one event in their routine awakens them to the mystery and wonder of existence and that is the creaking of the shed door, followed by the entrance of a human being.

At once all the cows are alert. Those lying down rise up on their forelegs; those already standing rush forward to the grille. Their normally vacant eyes are now awash with curiosity, and they push their wet muzzles through the bars as though offering them for sacrifice. Every movement of the man seems to entrance them; they know instinctively that he holds the key to both life and death. They do not necessarily like him; they are decidedly aware that he is not of their kind, and that he possesses powers, strengths and spells that they will never fathom and which will always overcome their feeble attempts at rebellion. But for that very reason they are consumed with interest in his actions, and are constantly trying to get him on their side. In short, they view him as a supernatural force, to be served, propitiated and worshipped.

The same is true of horses. Their phenomenal strength notwithstanding, horses are in awe of people, perpetually astonished by the human ability to outflank and defeat their simple strategies, and aware that all resistance to man's dominion is futile. The entrance of the groom into the stables is the signal for a general alertness, a struggling free from equine emotions towards the higher sphere of the supernatural. The horse consents to be mounted by a human being, and to surrender his will entirely to the thing above, because that thing is his true divinity.

Sheep respond in a similar way to the shepherd, and nobody who keeps a dog can doubt the underlying principle: although dogs recognize and give preference to their kind, they view people in general, and their owner in particular, as belonging to a higher order of being. We are their angels, and their human master is also their god. Indeed there is virtually no animal on the farm that does not give the lie to Xenophanes' sarcastic view of the religious instinct.

Of course, Xenophanes was right to point to the inherent paradox in viewing the gods as exaggerated humans. But this paradox is essential to theistic religion; after all, we have been offered no other example of the spiritual life. All that we witness of good and evil shows itself in human form, and, without the Biblical view that we are 'made in God's image', the moral nature of God – and therefore his fitness for worship – would be concealed from us. This is the thought that acquires uniquely credible expression in the Christian doctrine of the Incarnation.

There is one farmyard animal, however, that seems to live in a state of theological obtuseness from which no shock less than death will ever release it, and that is the chicken. Although I feed the chickens morn and night, releasing them by day and locking them up at sundown; although I prepare for them the most delicious and protein-rich porridge; although I clean their hut, give them fresh straw each week, and generally tend to their ailments and anxieties, they have continued to regard me in particular, and the human form in general, as unimportant accidents, of no more interest or concern than the rats that live beneath their hutch.

It is true that my actions have awoken in the chickens a profound habit of worship. But this worship is directed exclusively to my boots, which they follow with a slavish devotion, and which they try to propitiate with all the clucks and pecks and bows in their narrow repertoire. It matters not who wears the boots. For, in their invincible ignorance, the chickens thank not me but the boots for their food. They listen out all day for the squeak of those boots, and when they encounter them in the flesh, so to speak, they run joyfully towards them as though seeking salvation. Often I see them standing at the French windows of the library, lost in adoration of the boots which stand drying inside. Seeing them so hopelessly degraded by their idolatry I find it difficult to believe that these chickens are birds, descended down the same evolutionary tree as the hawk, the thrush and the nightingale – creatures that are symbols for us of the human spirit in its many guises, and the inspiration behind so many of our own visions of God.

Among the mysteries with which rural life confronts the incomer, birds and their cries are in fact the most unsettling – unsettling because settled in another and unhuman way. Soldiers reported from the trenches in the First World War that during every lull in the shelling they could hear rapturous birdsong. Death and destruction rained from the skies, but the skies themselves were full of music, as thrushes, blackbirds, larks and chaffinches staked out their ancestral claims to territory, indifferent to the human struggle to control it.

Something of the awe which those soldiers felt was visited upon us during the Foot and Mouth epidemic. The footpaths were closed, the fields deserted, the herds imprisoned and the farm gates closed.

One day the army came to shoot all the pregnant ewes on the hill, because their shepherd lived in an infected area. But it was spring, and above our heads the birds were seeking mates, claiming territory, and paying tribute to the life to come. We awoke each morning to their peaceful chorus – peaceful because it was not addressed to us, wanted nothing from us, and expressed a profound indifference to human hopes and troubles. When, after half an hour, baby Lucy too would awaken, we were shocked by the contrast between these songs that ignored us, and the new song aimed at our hearts.

Birdsong has a function. But the function explains none of its mystery. Why the decorative grace notes of the robin? Why the endless wasteful tunefulness of the nightingale, long after the point has been made? Why do some birds imitate, others learn, and some remain fixed for life in the musical groove of their parents? Birds don't sing as we do – for the sheer delight of it. But we hear music in their calls, and from time immemorial people have tried to capture this music in words. Some birds are named from their songs: the cuckoo, the pipit, the chiff-chaff, the curlew – whose name in Provençale (*le couroulu*) resembles the liquid flight with which bird seeks bird on the hillside. Sometimes we map the songs in words. 'To wit, to woo,' says the tawny owl; 'just a little bit of bread and no cheese', says the yellowhammer.

But all these attempts to lay a verbal graph across the raw material miss the unfathomable life of it. Nor do musicians fare much better. It is impossible to give musical notation for a real ecstatic birdsong. As I write a wren is booming from the treetops, throbbing like a piston engine as it drowns out every rival sound. It is a noise smeared over musical space and time, with neither beginning nor end: the very opposite of melody. And yet it is music to the ear: I imagine high repeated notes on flute and violin, and beneath them a running commentary from the percussion and an occasional thump on the 'cello.

Many composers have tried to give us the song of the nightingale: Couperin, Rameau, Handel, Schubert – even Brahms. But only fragments and echoes reward the attempt; Respighi gave up and introduced the bird itself into the orchestra – recorded and set among the woodwinds. And none of this compares with Keats's liquid *Ode*, in which the hidden melody is one of thought, not sound.

Only one musical work, in my experience, matches the tribute paid by Keats, and that is Messiaen's *Catalogue des oiseaux*. Messiaen's birds sing in huge six-voiced piano chords that range over the entire keyboard – an impossible feat for a single throat, and yet unmistakeably bird-like, with the supreme affirmation that we hear each spring morning from our window. Looking at the tiny throbbing wren, with her[15] throat wide open like a funnel and her tongue shaking as though from a hidden storm, I begin to understand what Messiaen was up to. These smeared sounds are really the close-packed upper harmonics of notes unheard in the bass – notes that live and breathe in hidden depths, and to which the wren bears witness in her confused ecstatic descant. Messiaen's chords explore the space below bird-song, the musical region which is occupied by no bird or man or animal, but by the soul of the universe itself.

There are two kinds of bird-song – the invariable cry of the species, and the inventive outpouring of the individual bird as it strives to mark out its territory. The song of a thrush, trying out phrases, discarding some, lingering over others and perfecting its favourites in a torrent of creative experiment, is, for us, the sound of repletion, of a creature at home in the world and rejoicing in its brief existence. To the thrush, of course, it is no such thing, but an unconscious need, just like everything else that crosses its tiny mind.

There is music in the high shrill whistle of the buzzard, in the owl's gloomy hoot, in the dove's syncopated monotone, and in the cuckoo's minor third. Even the dusty clatter of rooks has its atmosphere, giving emphasis to the tree-tops, and marking them out as a home. For me, however, the most beautiful of all the species-cries, and the one that bears the meaning of spring more completely than any other, is that of the stone-curlew. Compared with this soaring, liquid trill, the cuckoo's perfect interval is insipid and trite. Of course the cuckoo has inspired more music than the curlew. But the explanation is no tribute. Composers have used the cuckoo's two-note motive so as to make art and nature coincide: 'cuckoo' already has rhythmic, harmonic and melodic character. The curlew, by contrast, fills the air with a sound that has neither rhythm nor melody nor harmonic potential, a sound smeared over adjacent notes and musically indecipherable. It is a pure nature-sound, full of the urgency of species-life, as inexplicable to human ears as the sound of running water. Yet, in another sense, it contains more music than all the sounds of spring – more even than the skylark in its ecstatic cascade of tweets and twitters.

It is a sound suggestive of sea-spray, of the ripple of descending tides and the bubbling away of rock-pools. It is a sound so deeply foreign to our pastures that you sit up with a start when it first occurs, and wonder how it is that this stone-coloured visitor – with its long swelling shanks and delicate curved beak – should leave the sea-shore whose smooth texture it shares for the rough pasture of Braydon forest. It is as though a god of the oceans had come inland to mate with the earth: the call haunts the landscape, summoning the earth to renew itself and live again.

The curlew has another call besides its liquid trill – the glissando koor-li, rising by a fifth or more, which is commemorated in its name. The koor-li, unlike the high-pitched oscillating trill, can enter human music. You will hear it in Britten's *Curlew River* – the cry of the mad woman as she wanders in search of her dead son. This church parable, loosely based on a Noh play, though named from a river that flows in East Anglia, reminds us that, wherever the curlew hovers, so too do ghosts. The call that announces new life is also the voice of the dead. Such is the meaning of every species-cry; and it is a meaning that resounds as clearly in the koor-li as in the whoo-whoo-whooing of the owl. These species-cries speak to us from regions that the laws of human sympathy do not reach, where all is cold, law-governed and frozen by fate. Hence ornithologists tend to be the least sentimental of zoophiles, given to casting an impartial eye over their favourites and even to shooting them from the skies so as to study their finer features. Such was Gilbert White, who concludes his ardent description of the stone-curlew with the brutal sentence: 'After harvest I have shot them before the pointers in turnip-fields'.[16]

Such an attitude is far from that of the newcomer, who arrives in the country surrounded by a retinue of dogs and cats, and who believes that wild animals too should be protected as pets. Ten years in the country have persuaded me to the opposite view. When we direct our emotions towards creatures who cannot return them, it seems to me, we embroil ourselves in contradictions. These contradictions are epitomized by the domestic cat. With its sleek appearance, its clean and territorial habits, and its ability to simulate human love, the cat has secured an enviable niche in the household, exchanging phony sentiment for real food. But its banquets consist of other and less fortunate creatures, millions of whom are tortured into tins each day for the sake of our feline parasites.

Things were not always so. Cats were first domesticated because they had a job to do. And they were kept in a state of starvation, since a cat has to be fairly desperate before it will take on a farm-yard rat. By contrast our modern breeds confine their strictly recreational predations to the most timid and innocent of creatures: song-birds, field-mice, newts, frogs and butterflies, all of them useful to man and all of them vital to our fragile ecosystem. Our native wildlife is defenceless against the domestic cat, which was bred to be vicious towards everything smaller than itself, and which has secured the protection of its only potential enemy.

When our neighbour Jim went to his dream bungalow in Wales, he left his cats behind. Those cosy fireside purrs were rewarded at last with an unconditional rejection. For a while two half-wild felines prowled our neighbourhood, monopolizing the supply of small animals, and clearing the hedgerows of birds. The hawks and owls began to migrate to more hospitable places. Our efforts to restore the ecological balance were beginning to look increasingly futile, and the culprits didn't even have a fireside to warm or a lonely heart to console. They were destructive by-products of our human domination, a disease brought by man, from which man alone can defend himself.

Yet, in their own way, Jim's orphans were rather likeable: within a week or two they bore hardly a trace of their former hypocritical benevolence, and reassumed the opaque expression of their species. Watching them as they hunted along the verges, I was often moved to admiration for their alert, relentless, need-driven contempt for other living creatures – though when Roddy reported that they had met with an accident, I did not grieve.

Cats divide into the feral and the phony, dogs into working dogs and pets. In the countryside only working dogs are appreciated by people other than their owners. Pets, generally speaking, are a nuisance, and the more petted, the worse they are. One of our neighbours keeps a Jack Russell terrier called Poppy: a pampered, yapping, mud-spattering hooligan, who jumps at horses, probably kills chickens and appears unpredictably in the fields, setting everything in motion. Once a week Poppy asserts her 'right to roam' over our fields – and shows, incidentally, just what the consequence of the right to roam will be, when ramblers and their pets begin to comb the hillsides. Yapping hysterically as she pursues a scent along the hedgerows, Poppy scatters birds, rabbits and hares, frightens sheep, ignores all calls to order and sends the chickens running for refuge in obscure places from which they must be one by one retrieved. Why shouldn't she have her fun? her owner asks; she is only following her nature. But that is precisely what is wrong with her. A good dog is the dog who does *not* follow her nature, since she has acquired another and more useful one. Poppy forces the wildlife to use up its precious store of winter energy, drives the sheep through the fences, and upsets the routine of the farmyard.

Poppy should be compared with Tinker, another Jack Russell who belongs to Harry the rat-man. Tinker never appears except in the company of Harry, cradled beneath the lapel of an old brown duffle coat, his bright obedient face turned upwards to his master's. Tinker does not chase whatever his nature suggests, but only those things that his master commands. Until given the order, he stays obediently in his nest, uttering muted whines of anticipation, but leaving the rest to Harry. And Tinker has a job to do – a job that he alone can do efficiently.

The war between man and rat is ancient and endless. There are those who defend their barns and stores with anti-coagulant poisons. But such poisons inflict a terrible death; moreover they litter the barn, the ditches, and the nests with corpses that will poison other creatures in their turn, or else rot away and disgorge their venom into the waterways. From every point of view – practical, ecological and humanitarian – the rat-catcher is the right answer to the rat, and the best of ratters is a well-trained terrier.

No sooner is he put down on the floor of the barn, than Tinker disappears into the straw, finding tunnels and pockets that are all but invisible to the naked eye, and sending out muffled cries of excitement from beneath the rustling stack. Some of the rats flee before him, and for these Harry is waiting with his airgun. Others are down to Tinker, and although it is never good news to encounter the jaws of an enemy, there is no doubt that Tinker's rats have a better death than most wild animals, being despatched, as a rule, by a single bite through the spine. The job is done without demolishing the stack of straw, and without disturbing any creature save the miscreant. And thanks to Tinker Harry goes away with a much-needed tenner. Just as Harry is welcome because of Tinker, so is Tinker welcome because of Harry.

The relation between Harry and his dog is morally on a far higher level than that between the petter and the pet. Tinker earns his keep and is proud of it; Harry's love for him is steadfast, unsentimental and founded in an objective assessment of his qualities. They are companions-in-arms, whose mutual understanding is the result of their shared campaigns. And just as Tinker has been shaped by Harry, so has Harry by Tinker. Like Tinker he shuns superfluous speech and needless gestures. Like Tinker he focuses clearly and exactly on his prey, disregarding the calls of society until victory is won. His coat is a house for Tinker, and his earnings too are Tinker's.

Terriers get a bad press; but provide them with a use and you discover in them the very same virtues that we know from the sheepdog: fidelity, intelligence, an understanding of what is required of them, and above all a constant and self-renewing joy in their work. One local sheepdog makes a deep impression on those who observe him. His job is to herd cattle, not sheep, and the cattle under his charge must come in for milking at the busiest time of day, crossing the main road out of Malmesbury by the bridge known as Cow Bridge. The dog lies in the road, forcing the traffic to a halt and reproving any cow that is tempted to stray up the hill to the bright pastures beyond the town. Once the cows have crossed, he ushers them down a narrow passage to the old stone farmhouse, which stands back-to-back with a microchip factory. More than the farm itself, more than the fields and the river Avon which waters them, this dog is a symbol of the boundary between town and country, defying the motor-mania of the highway and the self-engendered haste of the town, toiling with steadfast and focused labour, indifferent to everything in his vicinity save the cows that define his task.

Of course, such a dog will sit by the fire with his owner, just like the pet; and he too will receive caresses. Unlike the pet, however, he is not there to give proof that his owner is lovable. He is there because he has earned his place in the domestic economy and proved himself a friend. That is why the sight of Harry and Tinker together is so affecting: their emotion is focused not on each other, but on the common task. It is a true comradeship, of the kind that men experience in battle. This battle has shaped their life, and they are fortunate that it is a battle that can never be won.

Generally speaking we have taken a tolerant attitude to our rats, merely flushing them from the barns from time to time, and shutting them out of the house. One summer night, however, I awoke to a crash downstairs, and went down to discover the remains of our supper on the kitchen floor. The lively marital discussion that ensued was inconclusive as to the crucial question, of who left open the library door. But there was nothing for it but to defend our territory. Unfortunately rats are able to maintain total silence, sniffing the air in some secret corner until sure that the enemy has left the scene, and only then venturing forth on their work of destruction. All day we poked gingerly in corners. And when night came without a sign of the intruder we assumed that he had gone back home.

And indeed he had done so. For his home was now beneath our kitchen. Next morning, after clearing away the remains of a bag of flour, we discovered a hole in the skirting board, where the rat had gnawed through and disappeared into the stone foundations. Henceforth terriers, cats, clubs and airguns would all be useless. Nor could we keep vigil by his hole, since the presence of a human sentinel would simply cause him to make another one.

We sealed up all the food, in the hope of starving him out. But always he found some sustenance, if only from chewing a coat or a carpet. After a week we were in despair. For there is no way in which you can share your home with a real farmyard rat. By this time he had eaten the edges of the kitchen linoleum, the skirting under the larder door, the plastic legs off the baby's high chair, the heel of a boot, two sou'westers, and a volume of Burke, one of a formerly complete set of eight. One night I awoke to the familiar crash, reached for the light, and found that the house was without electricity. The rat had gnawed through one of the cables, an experience that he had taken, like every other, in his stride.

It was clear that it was either us or him. We summoned the pest-control officer, who agreed that there was nothing for it but poison. All principles – humane, ecological, political, scientific – were thrown to the winds, and the lethal packets stowed behind the skirting.

We lay awake, half remorseful, half eager for news. But for several nights there was silence. The poison remained untouched, the house undisturbed, except for small signs here and there, as though the rat had wandered from room to room in search of a lost companion. Then, one night, we heard a distant sawing and scraping and thrashing – signs, we imagined, that the poison was now at work. Only when the noise suddenly stopped did we lapse into a fitful and guilty sleep.

The next morning we discovered that the frame of the living room window had been eaten through, the glass dislodged, and a hole created that was big enough for a cat to pass. To our astonishment, the rat had escaped – poison untouched, and all claim to our territory abandoned. Clearly his presence in our house had been a mistake – a mistake that he regretted even more than we did. He had fed himself for a while; but his heart was elsewhere, in the stinking ditches where his family lived, and in the warm muck-heap full of worms.

And let's face it: in the battle between us, the rat had won, expertly destroying both the house and its peace. The sum total of the damage, including the cost of a new window-frame, was £1,000; the household insurance policy does not cover the effects of vermin; and even today neither of us will admit to that wide-open library door.

The rat is not the only pest whose numbers have vastly increased as a result of our assaults on the natural order. Crows and magpies now dominate our hedgerows, preying on the nests of more melodious birds, and only the jay – unique among the corvids in being beautiful to look at – has suffered a decline. The grey squirrel continues to establish its empire in the woods, and the feral cat and the fox are now taking charge of our gardens.

The best answer to a pest is to encourage the predator that will eat it. And the most efficient predator is man. The way to re-establish ecological balance, therefore, is to acquire the habit of eating your competitors. Such at least is Don's opinion, and in our pub Don's opinion carries a weight of authority far beyond his 30 years. An odd-job man by trade and by nature, Don has lived in these parts all his life, inheriting his father's mobile home, and now hoping, if the Council will let him, to build a house of his own. He knows the woods, the fields and the farms for miles around, and is welcome everywhere for his skills. Don can build, plumb, wire, join, shoot and trap; no vehicle is too far gone for Don to have a go at mending it, and no land too rough, wet or barren for Don to work. He knows the birds and beasts of the fields and woodlands, their habitats, customs and uses. And he is an expert on all the deeper matters that are pondered in our pub on a Friday night: ale, weed-killer, dragonflies, distributor caps, interest rates, cider, sugar beet, brass bands, planning law and newts.

In the heart of Great Wood there is an ancient colony of red squirrels – holding out against the greys with all the courage and ingenuity of the Texans at El Alamo. Don goes to watch them flicker in the branches, as bright in this grey-green habitat as parrots in a jungle or fireworks in the midnight sky. And he takes his gun – a .22 rifle – hoping to turn it on their grey oppressors. There was a time when the Government offered a shilling for every grey squirrel pelt. Now the business of controlling the invader is left to private enterprise. But, says Don, if people knew what they were missing, these pests would disappear tomorrow.

Red squirrels have a foul gland next to the kidney which ruins their taste. The greys, however, are sweet and succulent. You need four per person, in Don's estimation – not because they are particularly small, but because they are surpassingly delicious, redder and more gamey than rabbit, but less pungent than muntjac or hare. The squirrel should be skinned and eviscerated. You should leave the head on, not only because the cheeks are a special delicacy, but also because it serves the same ornamental function as the head of a sea bass or a woodcock. Don't take out the eyes, but leave them to cloud over like opals in the heat of the fire. Marinate the squirrel for a few hours in olive oil, with salt, pepper and a squeeze of lemon juice; then skewer the length of its body and grill on both sides.

As troublesome as the squirrel, and sharing its habitat, is the rook – a nest-robber and scavenger whose population is constantly on the verge of explosion. Like other corvids, the rook is a rapid learner, and a confident exploiter of its dominant niche. Once a year, around the middle of May, our people gather on an evening for the shoot, assembling beneath the 'rooky wood' in their camouflage, and opening fire with shotguns when the young birds – new to the danger and destined, if they survive, to flee it forever after – come home to roost.

After the barrage the carcasses are gathered up, and the feast prepared. Only young rooks will do for Don's pie: beyond their first year the birds are as wiry and rasping as their name, and should be left for the foxes. You don't pluck the rook but skin it, detaching the breasts, which are plump, red and flavoursome like the breasts of pigeons, and placing them in a pie dish. When the dish is three-quarters full cover with a thick layer of sliced hard-boiled eggs, anoint with stock, add a pinch of nutmeg and bake in a pie-crust for an hour and a half.

As much a pest as the rook and the squirrel is the deer. During my first years of settling I took Wallace Stevens' view that these delicate creatures, arising from the grass like a sudden visitations, are part of earth's glory:

> Deer walk upon our mountains, and the quail
> Whistle about us their spontaneous cries.

However, our mountains are merely the top of Sundey Hill, and the copse that we planted there is being steadily consumed.

One day, when we had discovered a whole spinney vandalized and were at our wits' end for a remedy, Mervyn presented himself. He had been here before, in the company of his old comrades from the army. Dressed in baggy camouflage, with a large knife at his waist and an assortment of guns across his shoulder, Mervyn is the one his mates turn to for the gruesome jobs – skinning, gutting, or the *coup de grâce*. And he looks the part, with a face like a wrinkled leather handbag, from which a few ornamental shark's teeth still hang by a thread.

A man of few words but fierce loyalties, Mervyn is typical of the new countryman. Living as he does on a small army pension, after active service in the forgotten war that saved Oman, Mervyn cannot afford to live where his heart is. He commutes in his battered Subaru from Swindon, installing himself in the fields and hedgerows, and performing what little services will bring him into contact with creatures more speechless than himself. He does not respond to your call; like the weather and the wildlife, he occurs.

There he was, just when we needed him, standing fully armed at the door, looking away, as is his manner, at some distant commotion on the hillside, and mumbling something about muntjacs. 'Take them on if you like,' he said, patting his rifle. Our problem, I told him, is the roe deer. He shook his head sagely. 'Roe's no harm,' he said, 'not here. It's the muntjacs. I seen they done for them willows you planted.' I felt a surge of relief on hearing this, since I trust Mervyn's judgement, and not only because it happened to coincide with mine. The real nuisances in our countryside are animals that are too small to see, too cunning to shoot, or too prolific to cull. Often they are imports from foreign parts, like the grey squirrel, the mink or the muntjac. Of Asian origin (the name is from Javanese *mindjangan*) muntjacs escaped a century ago from Woburn Abbey park, and, like the mink, found a disused ecological niche and entered it with all the force of a drug-pusher in a children's playground. You need a rifle to kill them, but they run through the long grass or the undergrowth, and are seldom a visible target. Only a calm, patient countryman of the old school can provide the time, the steady hand and the immovable depth of silence that will eventually spell their death.

Mervyn came back that evening with one of the culprits, and hung it in the barn. Next day he returned with his knife; the muntjac was skinned and jointed, and the forequarters put into a marinade of red wine, onions, herbs, juniper and garlic. Living muntjac is deer at its worst – verminous, sneaky and in ruthless competition with our native species. But dead muntjac is friendly to man, with the flavour and the texture of hare – strong, dark, but also tender and gelatinous. Jugged muntjac is the perfect dish to set before bambi-lovers, a dish that reeks of the wild and of the life that teems in it. It reminds us that we can make a truce with deer, but no lasting settlement.

Don and Mervyn exemplify a healthy form of environmental activism, taking local action against local pests, and trying to restore equilibrium in a small but neighbourly patch. Nation-wide attempts to rectify human damage are often less successful. The problem is illustrated by the invention of the 'protected species', usually in response to the favouritism that comes from dividing animals into pests and pets.

Certain animals can be dressed in Beatrix Potter costumes and sat down in some imaginary domestic haven. It helps if they have bright eyes and fur. Length of leg is also a factor, as is colour and the flesh of the tail. Rats fail on most counts: their scuttling movements, lightless coat, and raw pink tails mark them down for persecution. Even rats, however, can be dressed in skirts for Beatrix Potter purposes, and their near relative the water vole became, thanks to *The Wind in the Willows*, a much loved English character. It is an irony of fate that the water vole should have been destroyed by animal-lovers, who, in a fit of habitual self-righteous anger against their own human kind, released the bright-eyed mink from its captivity. But it is a good illustration of the damage done to animals by our unthinking partisanship.

Chief favourite among the wild mammals of Britain is the badger, who, like his cousin the bear, plays a starring role in children's stories. The badger's roomy sett is indeed a set of rooms. Here the animals come in their neatly buttoned trousers to sip tea and discuss the ways of man, their common enemy. Immortalized by the enchantment of childhood, they become imaginary companions thereafter. We carry them within us in a death-denying Eden, a place of innocence, where 'every prospect pleases, And only man is vile'. (How immeasurably superior to all this English whimsy is Janáček's great animal opera, *The Cunning Little Vixen*, which restores death to its central place in the drama.)

In recognition of his endearing texture the badger has become a protected species. Our badger population is now thought to be awash with diseases, and may very well be responsible for the escalation of bovine TB, which last year claimed ten of the cows on our farm. Moreover, a sett can stretch into the middle of a field, endangering horses, vehicles and cattle, and almost every week we hear of an accident. Sophie's horse trod in a sett one morning, somersaulted over her, and left her bruised and trampled; I broke a collar bone the same way. Two years ago a nearby farmer was killed when the ground gave way beneath his tractor. Sometimes at dusk a badger scouts the pasture by our house, sniffing for field-mice. Seeing him thus, ruthless, intent and in his element, I acknowledge him as an enemy to be respected. And always it saddens me to find the body of a badger on the road. But neither the ruthless hunter nor the crumpled victim has ever worn trousers.

Some people fear that the badger problem may be reproduced by the otter, an equally vicious and equally beautiful creature, lovingly, if sentimentally, celebrated by Gerald Durrell, and now being introduced, in colonies of 17 at a time, into the Thames. George, who has a trout farm on a tributary of that river not far from here, dreads the day when the otters reach his banks. Once the good news of free eating is relayed from whisker to whisker down the Thames, George believes that he will be forced to say goodbye to his livelihood. If he fights back, he will face criminal charges; and if he doesn't, nobody will compensate his loss.

Maybe George's fears are exaggerated: only when the otters have re-established their hold will we know. What is certain, however, is that the idea of a 'protected species' is as much an intrusion into the natural order as the agricultural methods it is designed to rectify. Many ponds are being fished to lifelessness by herons. It is true that you can obtain a licence to shoot a heron, if it is a serious threat to your fish; but that does nothing for the ecological balance of the ponds that really matter – those fragile dewponds which are to all intents and purposes unowned and unseeded, and where our native water-life struggles to survive in something like its natural condition.

Our own little stretch of muddy water began life as a dewpond, but was enlarged and stocked with carp by my predecessor at Sunday Hill Farm. It is known as Iris pond, from the time when John Bailey and Iris Murdoch were discovered swimming there, stark naked, happy as children, their folds of pink flesh smeared with dark brown mud and their mouths open in song – 'For the rain it raineth every day', as I recall, one of their ample repertoire of Shakespeare lyrics. Probably this was the only time in recent years when the three herons who have been challenging each other with raucous cries over the right to fish in our pond have kept a proper distance from it.

Herons are said to migrate in the winter, but surely not very far: at the first breath of spring, when little clouds of mud are the only sign that the fish are stirring on the bottom, the herons are back, flying straight across woods and fields, and swerving onto the ponds with hungry mutterings. For hours on end they stand in the shallows, grey and motionless as stones. And at nightfall they flap away, part of our harvest entombed in their bills.

In our vague plans to diversify we imagine ourselves in the role of carp-farmers, furnishing a commodity that is increasingly rare, now that the oceans are being pillaged without scruple: mature fish, freshly landed, their job of reproduction finished, and their small chance of contentment seized. A great work of education is needed, however, if the English are ever to appreciate the merits of carp. Second among freshwater fish only to the pike in flavour, the carp shares with that sinister predator the detached and disagreeable bones that lodge in its fleshiest part. East Europeans are able to suck the flesh from these bones and to spit them out without revulsion. Twenty years of travel in Eastern Europe have taught me that this skill must be acquired early if it is to be acquired at all. The solution is to treat carp as pike are treated by *haute cuisine*: namely as fish that are served either cold in their own firm jelly, in quenelles, or in a soup, from which they are lifted and de-boned during cooking.

Last summer I caught one in a net, conscious of the unsporting nature of what I did, but rejoicing nevertheless in my triumph. I was re-living a boyhood dream: I was bringing a big fish home, and I myself had caught it! But alas, the trophy would not die. Blows to the head merely intensified its reproachful stare, and redoubled its efforts to leap from the table. I thought of a tray of carp that I had seen in the Chinese market in New York, gasping piteously after many hours, and seeming to beg each passer-by to release them from their suffering. But then I remembered the carp-vendor in the streets of old Budapest, who would take the wriggling fish from his tank and in less than 10 seconds hand it over as neatly severed segments in a roll of newspaper. I went to the woodshed for the axe and applied myself to the task.

Three hours and five drinks later, my victim, steeped in white wine and relieved of its bones, lay cooling in a pâté dish. Only a few teaspoonfuls remained of the leviathan that I had wrestled from the water. But I was confident that it would taste all the better for being so severely reduced. The green slime that appeared next day at table, tasting of mud, shoe-polish and rancid butter, convinced me that there is more to carp-farming than meets the eye. I understood that the real relation between Englishman and carp – the relation that guarantees the future of our pond-life – is a relation of sport, not need. We decided, therefore, that the correct use of Iris pond is as a resort for anglers.

The poet, diplomat and compleat angler Sir Henry Wotton said of his sport (according to Izaak Walton) that it was 'an employment for his idle time, which was then not idly spent ... a rest to his mind, a cheerer of his spirits, a diverter of sadness, a calmer of unquiet thoughts, a moderator of passions, a procurer of contentedness; and that it begat habits of peace and patience in those that professed and practised it.'[17] Observing the use of Iris pond, I would add another, and to my thinking far more important, attribute to the list of angling's virtues.

Fishing brings father and son together, in the kind of silent masculine intentness that uniquely ties the paternal bond. Although I do not fish, I have observed this process in the men who come to Iris pond: in Adam the farrier, Nathan the builder, and Roger the window-cleaner. All of them bring their young boys, so as to enjoy those hours of silence side by side, their minds emptied of troubles and their hearts of conflict, their four eyes focused on the float.

For man and boy to do exactly the same thing for three hours, that thing must be a no-thing, a cessation, during which the separate rhythms of their bodies can slow to a single pulse, and their separate thoughts be pooled in one all-dissolving interest. This intent, silent, pursuit of the quarry reaches deep into the hunter-gatherer soul. And from the reservoir of archaic feeling is drawn the tenderest affection that a father can know. Angling seems to provide men with a moment when they can love their sons silently and without embarrassment, and know that they are loved in turn. To my mind this is a sufficient vindication.

Angling is not good for the fisherman only. It is good for the fish. Those who worry about the welfare of hunted animals tend to look on the down-side of what we do to them. But fish are destined to suffer, come what may: the fish that is never caught will one day die from predation, pollution, starvation or disease. And where fish are hunted for sport they have the benefit of human protection. We now feed the carp in Iris pond, drive away the herons and cormorants, keep vigil against pollution, and maintain the surrounding ecosystem. Angling, unlike drift-netting, targets the individual, and leaves, or ought to leave, the rest of nature unaffected. Moreover it is a sport, guided by rules and procedures, and by a duty of care towards the quarry. That is another reason why father and son meld together by the pond: one is silently teaching, and the other silently learning the rules of engagement.

Although our attempts to feed ourselves from Iris pond came to nothing, we have had better luck with Braydon Pond, at the top of our hill. Here lies a thriving shooting estate, purchased by a Belgian industrialist following a ban on sport shooting in his homeland, and run by Malcolm, the gamekeeper. Malcolm keeps his neighbours supplied throughout the season with partridge, teal, widgeon, mallard and pheasant. Unlike supermarket chickens, his pheasants have run wild and free, have done all the things that their nature requires, and have died in a sudden plunge to earth of which they knew little or nothing. If you are worried, as you ought to be, about the sufferings of the animals you eat, then eat wild duck, partridge or pheasant, and you will be on the side of the angels.

However, you must hang a pheasant for ten days before plucking it. You must remove the feathers carefully, without breaking the skin. And you must snap the shanks of the legs and tear off the feet, so pulling out the tendons, whose toughness bears witness to a happy life in the woods and hedgerows. All this means that you won't find a proper pheasant at your local butchers – certainly not one with that tempting grass-green tint that signifies the ripe stage of putrefaction.

Purists will argue that these flamboyant birds do not count as wildlife: after all, the gamekeeper reared them. Moreover, they are not native to this country, but were brought from China in the early Renaissance, their Greek name being derived from the river Phasis in ancient Colchis, where a similar bird inhabited the meadows. Pheasants are merely hand-reared ornamental chickens, that happen to fly if they really feel they must. But that is precisely why we should appreciate them. They are a living proof that human beings can live in harmony with other species, can protect them, maintain their habitats, and still allow them the luxury of being wild.

The point was brought home to me by our rabbits: gregarious animals, for whom there is only one mental torture greater than solitary confinement, which is that of being cuddled by a member of a large rabbit-eating species. The pet rabbit learns to adapt to its conditions, much as human beings learned to adapt to Stalin's gulag. Being unable to shift its eyes, it maintains its generous stare even when held by a smelly omnivore emitting vile drooling noises, and smiling down on it from a mouth full of teeth. Correct behaviour is rewarded, after all, with a piece of lettuce. In this way the rabbit teeters from terror to terror and from day to day.

In the wild, however, in the teeming burrow where he mates promiscuously with his kind, where the only smell is the smell of rabbit and where every intruder is regarded with abhorrence, the rabbit takes his revenge for the torment suffered by his domesticated cousin: eating crops, destroying saplings, and undermining paths and fields. The solution to this problem was introduced by James, our blacksmith's apprentice, who took me aside one day and asked, in a conspiratorial tone of voice, whether it would be alright for him and a few of the boys to bring their ferrets round. The conspiratorial tone, I discovered, is essential to the art of ferreting, as are cloth caps, tough jackets, bite-proof gloves, and a general air of intense concentration.

The ferret is as furry and appealing to the sight as a rabbit, and would feature in children's books, in some toothless version, were it not for the fact that nobody knows anything about it except those who know everything, and who love the ferret with the severe military love that attaches the falconer to his bird and the huntsman to his hounds. Such a one is James, who lifts his precious animal from its box as though handling a new-born baby, and who coos to it quietly in a private language far richer in syllables than the sparse dialect that he keeps for human use. And when he slips the ferret into the warren and watches it slide into the darkness, his face is full of a tender anxiety, like the face of a father whose son is leaving for the wars.

Nets have been staked over the exits, and the bystanders drop to the ground and listen. The ensuing silence is the silence of the hunter-gatherer – an intense communion with nature, a knowledge that death has suddenly moved into position on the edge of things, and is about to show his hand. All of a sudden the warren begins to throb; there is a violent drumming sound, the earth seems to heave and tremble as though at the approach of an earthquake, and after a second or two the rabbits tumble into the light. Their convulsive movements are full of a primordial terror – not the daily, debilitating anxiety of the captive pet, but the salutory terror that ensures the strength and survival of a species. In this case, however, terror is of no avail. The rabbits are caught in the net, and quickly dispatched with a stick. The ferret is rewarded with the heads: the skinned torsos are kept for the pot.

The hunter-gatherer's way of obtaining food is epitomised by ferreting and falconry, in which people hunt side by side with animals, in the same free spirit and with the same view of territory.[18] The livestock farmer, by contrast, deals with animals who have already been marked out as food, taken into possession, and alloted a temporary tenancy on the farm. These are settled animals, and none epitomizes them more effectively than the pig: a species that could not exist were it not for the elaborate process of domestication that has engineered it to our uses. It is one of the great mysteries, to my mind, that this animal, created by us, should also be so vehemently condemned by us, and for the very use for which we created him. In the dietary laws of Leviticus the pig is denounced as unclean. The judgement is repeated in the Koran. So great was the horror aroused by the flesh of the pig in the old semitic peoples that the Apostle Peter needed a divine vision, inspired by extreme hunger, before he could break the taboo (Acts 10:10). But why should God have taken against pig-eating? The question has occupied the waking hours of a thousand theologians and anthropologists, but so far with no sign of a persuasive answer.

The pig was created for the table. He is omnivorous, a perfect way of recycling human leftovers, and at the same time a tame and obliging member of the household. He has translucent sensitive skin which bears witness to the abundant sweet flesh beneath it. His eyes are half-closed, emitting no doe-eyed glances with which to stay the hand of his executioner. His one defence is a squeal so high-pitched as to invite the final punishment. He also *looks* like food: a round, plump offering on sticks, ready at any moment to lose his individuality and slide down the metaphysical ladder from thing to stuff.

And of course, he tastes good, and just about every bit of him is edible. He is the source of *charcuterie*, the highest of all culinary art-forms. There is surely no tastier morsel than the dried and shrivelled, layered and self-stuffed, re-incombobulated intestine of a porker, spiced with garlic and caraway, smoked over a wood fire and served up as *andouillettes*. How could a reasonable God, concerned for his human creatures, forbid us to feast ourselves on such things? It doesn't make sense.

At least it doesn't make sense to us here, in the Wiltshire claylands, where we are bound to the pig by an ancient covenant. Like our Gloucestor Old Spots, Brian's Tamworths enjoy the old life of the family porker, sleeping on straw and rummaging in open stalls, eating a mixed and varied swill of apples, grain, milk and leftovers. Brian spends many a spare hour with the pigs, for they are amusing companions and relate easily to their human keepers, whom they always greet with a cry of recognition and an enquiring grunt. Although their conversation is limited, it compares favourably with that of today's school-leavers, and their simple pleasure in being scratched behind the ears is an equal pleasure in the one who causes it. On Brian's farm, where girls from Swindon keep their horses, where cows gather at the gates, and where dogs and children visit every corner of the yard, the pigs do not suffer from boredom, but do their best to join in the fun. Peggy, the breeding sow, is a particular favourite, and honks at every passer-by to gain attention.

Alas Malmesbury slaughterhouse, famous for two Tamworth pigs that once escaped from it, to become thereafter expensive charges on the public purse, has not survived the Euro-madness, and Snowball and Napoleon, our first experiments in pig-keeping, had to be taken to the slaughterhouse in Calne. Snowball, the first to go, went quietly. Napoleon, however, who had grieved over his companion and deduced his fate, refused to enter the trailer until lassooed and winched in with a rope.

The stress of transportation, to an animal that guesses how the ordeal will end, ought to be a cause of scandal. And the chopping factory likewise, though for different reasons. I petitioned in vain for Snowball's blood, trotters and intestines, and although the head and liver were delivered at last to the factory door, something in the frozen half-smile that looked up at me from the bloody packet suggested that this was not the Snowball with whom I had exchanged so many greetings.

The factory processing of the pig wastes half of him, and the better half too. We have therefore decided to join the criminal classes, and butcher our current charges – Ryder and Singer – at home. We are already recruiting the neighbours to the task, and they are looking forward to it, recalling the pig-keeping culture that shaped their countryside and to which their parents and grandparents belonged. Language itself reminds us of this culture: to lead someone up the garden path or by the nose are idioms derived from those last moments of a pig's life, when it is taken to the place of slaughter. Pig-killing was a ceremony, a ritual sacrifice, in which the whole community joined, to create the puddings, pies, hams and jellies that made use of every part. The Czech word for December is *Prosinec* – pig-killing – since December was the time when every household harvested its sausages. And still in our nursery rhymes the little piggies have an honoured if tragic place.

Breeds used to vary from place to place and town to town. Only recently did our local Old Wessex Saddleback give way to the Gloucester Old Spot and the Tamworth. Despite the dominance of the Large White, and the gradual relegation of all other breeds to the category of the exotic, the pig retains his primeval fascination. Sometimes you see an old man pause at a gate where a pig is visible, not to consider the creature's merits, but to refresh himself with the memory of an ancient relation between species, and to enjoy a silent dialogue whose rhythms have entered the folk memory. For the pig is a symbol of the self-sufficient cottager. Man and pig shared their simple life, and possessed the land together.

Pigs cannot easily be herded, since they dodge, swerve and bound towards you, sometimes moving with such speed and energy as to knock you down. Although the swineherd is familiar from Homer, and crops up in Anglo-Saxon literature, I doubt that he did much herding. In fact the pig and his sty convey a simple message, which is that we are not moving but settling, and this place is ours. We share that feeling, and have built our sty of natural stone, with a Romanesque arch for a door and a roof of Roman tiles. Looking at the contented forms of Ryder and Singer as they snore inside I can understand why pig-keeping got up the Jewish nose. The Semitic tribes were shepherds, who conceived the pastoral way of life as a revelation of God's purpose and as God's way with the landscape. Their rage against the pig was prompted by the sight of people already settled in the promised land, who were determined to defend it against the invader, God or no God. The pigs that rootled and snorted in the farmyards of those settled people were the most vivid proof of their prescriptive right. To denigrate the swineherd and to exalt the shepherd were therefore both required by a propaganda war.

The most beautiful by-product of that war was the Hebrew Bible. Images of nomadic flocks form the soothing, shifting background to the Old Testament Psalms. Largely because of sheep, therefore, our ancestors learned that human nature is permanent and universal, the same in ancient Palestine as in the Cotswolds. When the wool trade became the cornerstone of the European economy, sheep provided the wealth of England. Towns grew on the back of sheep, as did the styles of English architecture. Tudor monarchs owed their power and culture to the flocks that carpeted the hillsides, and it was thanks to wool, and the fulling, dyeing and weaving that are needed to make use of it, that markets began to grow into industrial towns.

The mark of this wool trade can be discerned everywhere around us, and most vividly in the wool towns themselves. Because they grew at a time when people built in stone and with pious regard for the look and the longevity of everything they did, these towns are as beautiful as any towns in England. This is evidenced by Malmesbury and also – rather more grandly – by Tetbury, whose wonderful church, one of the few examples of Georgian Gothic still surviving, dominates the countryside for miles around. Tetbury was the centre of commerce, festivity and religion for the sheep farms of the southern Cotswolds. Once a year it would put itself on display by means of a peculiar late-medieval institution: the woolsack race.[19] Young farmers would compete for prizes by running up the one-in-four gradient of Gumstool Hill, carrying 60-pound sacks of wool on their shoulders. So doing they also impressed the crowds of admiring maidens and sometimes even came away with a bride. The streets were crowded with young and old, the town wore a festive face, and the inns stayed open until all had drunk their fill.

Then, in Thomas Hardy's day, the wool-trade collapsed, and the institution of the woolsack race disappeared. For many local people the death-sentence had been passed on Tetbury, and there was nothing for it but to watch the town decay.

For a while Tetbury did decay. The sheep farms broke up, the young men were sucked into the death machine of the Great War, and the young women drifted to the cities. But then, in the sixties, new industries began to settle on the edge of the town, enjoying commercial facilities that had remained intact during the years of depression. The surrounding landowners, many of them with city interests, renewed their custom, and the town revived. Twenty-seven years ago the corporation decided to bring back the woolsack race. Each summer bank holiday the streets are again crowded with people, who come from all over the district to watch the sweating contestants as they stagger up the slope of Gumstool Hill. Women too compete, bearing lighter sacks, and one of them – a Malmesbury schoolteacher – carried off last year's prize. The contest is open to outsiders too: the team event was won by the Royal Ghurka Rifles, and those serene Nepalese faces, showing scarcely a sign of effort, found a perfect setting in the cliff-like facades of Cotswold stone between which they ran, as though carrying stores up a mountain path in the Himalayas.

When the wool trade flourished sheep would be kept for as long as they could profitably be sheared. Hence arose the national dish of Johnson's and Jane Austen's days: roast mutton and onion sauce. Today there is no economic reason to prolong the life of a sheep: what the butcher sells as lamb is really sheep too young to have acquired the rank flavour, somewhere between venison and dish-cloth, which is the true essence of mutton. Sheep, which were once the greatest source of national wealth, have become a symbol of poverty. Hill farmers can now barely afford the cost of slaughtering their animals. And the sheep that we see in our valley are often temporary tenants of the fields where they graze, brought in lorry-loads by Welsh farmers, who pay what they can to winter their flocks in sheltered regions before moving them back to the hills.

In our neighbourhood, however, sheep are residents as well as seasonal migrants, and lambing is one of the most important seasons of the year, when farmers must not only assist in scores of births but also watch out for orphaned or rejected lambs. For a brief moment the farmer fills the role of the Good Shepherd. One orphan was found by Paul, our next door neighbour's young son, a few years ago. The lamb had been out all night, and had been caught and worried by a dog. Alive but bleeding, he had been brought into the kitchen, and his wounds sewn up. Each day Paul would feed him with cow's milk from a bottle and in due course he recovered. He acquired a name – Herbie – and was the playmate and daily companion of his rescuer. The children of the neighbourhood were all drawn to Herbie, and he would frisk and skip with them quite happily as though they too were lambs and as though no harm could ever come to him in such joyful company.

And then, one day, Herbie ceased to dance. He observed the gambols of his former playmates from the zig-zag pupils of his yellowing eye with a cool and cynical disdain. He responded to the small hands that patted and caressed him with barely concealed impatience. At every opportunity he sought to melt into the anonymous fleece on the hillside, and to drift with the tide of collective fear or frenzy. He had lost his personality, and become a sheep. A few months later we ate Herbie, not shedding a tear.

Sheep are more likely to survive in our neighbourhood than cows. Their only defect in the farmer's eyes is their ability to find holes in hedges and to decant like a fluffy liquid from field to field. Otherwise they can be left out in all but the most inclement weather. Moreover they have a role in the new equestrian culture that links the rural heartlands to the towns.

This culture has been the saviour of our community, the one source of reliable profit in times of deep uncertainty. Many of our farmers deal in horses, hire out stables as 'do-it-yourself' liveries, let grass-keep for hunters over the summer, and offer livery service in the winter. Our neighbour, Alf, also uses his cattle-truck to collect and deliver horses in the area. The equestrian side of his business employs two people, and provides odd jobs and part-time occupations for those who come and go in the stables. Indeed, thanks to horses, Alf is the only farmer nearby who offers work outside his own family circle.

Alf heals the rift between town and country. Urban people who keep their horses on his farm see what is happening in the countryside, and form ties of friendship with the locals. Alf meanwhile protects the landscape from their animals. Fields grazed by horses soon become clumpy with couch grass, nettles, thistles, docks and boopoles. Unless sheep are brought in to graze off the coarser plants, the fields will become horse-sick, and unfit for pasture. Only if horses are kept by farmers, therefore, do they cease to be an ecological threat.

The animals raised in Alf's yard show no fear of sheep, pigs, chickens, ducks, dogs or tractors, and are immune even to the inter-continental lorries that his brother-in-law drives in from time to time off the motorway, and which often end their lives as horse-boxes. Everything that happens to them – grooming, shoeing, boxing, hunter trials, hacks and fun rides – happens in an atmosphere of easy-going species-life, a life shared with other animals and with people, punctuated by familiar routines and enlivened by the sounds and smells of the farmyard. Such horses are the safest of rides, and the easiest of companions. And they form the primary matter of our equestrian way of life – a way of life that is an essential ingredient in the identity and history of the English people.

There are close on a million horses and ponies in private ownership in Britain. It has been plausibly argued that the friendship between our species is the reason why they have both survived.[20] Whole classes of British people still exist for whom equine company is a necessity, and when they find themselves trapped in the suburbs, their horses and ponies come to join them in the paddock next door. The horse breeds clubs, competitions and festivals that bring people together more firmly than perhaps any rival form of social life. The Pony Club, with its events and camps and holidays; the hunter trials and point-to-points; the cross-country rides and pony treks; the shows, gymkhanas and three-day events; the National hunt races and the Grand National – all illustrate our genius for institution building. Country life in Britain is full of social events to which children look forward and in which adults can rediscover childhood. And the root cause of this is the horse.

Gracious manners and formal dress are the norm, whether at the gymkhana, in the Pony Club or at cross-country events. This formality is integral to the discipline required of the rider, and is at the same time a mark of respect for the horse, who is raised above his species-being by grooming and polishing, so as to meet his rider on equal terms.

Anthropologists have argued that societies are bound together by rites of passage – by ceremonies, titles and sacramental ordeals whereby people pass from one state to another within the community. Some rites occur at birth, others at marriage, others still at death. But most important are those that signify 'coming of age' – the acquisition of adult status, and the assumption of the duties and privileges of a grown-up. For these are the rituals that cause young people to identify with the past and future of their society and which are the foundation of social renewal.

This need for rites of passage is still met in equestrian communities. There is a continuous apprenticeship, through dressage, eventing, show-jumping and hunting, requiring a gradual increase in courage and a step-by-step submission to the laws and conventions of the equestrian culture. And the child emerges from this apprenticeship emancipated from minority, a fully-fledged member of the tribe. That is the real reason why so many farmers keep horses. Through horses their children graduate to rural life, acquire the virtues and manners of society, and yet remain attached to the farm and to those (including the animals) who live there.

There is one rural gathering entirely devoted to this process of initiation – and that is the Pony Club. The Pony Clubs were established by the hunts in the wake of the First World War. Most serviceable horses had been requisitioned for the battle front, and few survived. People were becoming habituated to motor traffic, and the tractor was rapidly displacing the horse from its traditional position in the farm. A conscious policy seemed necessary, if young people were to acquire the knowledge and the interest that would perpetuate the equestrian culture of the English countryside. Like the Scout movement that arose from the South African war, the Pony Club rapidly grew beyond its original purpose, acquiring a uniform, a discipline, an ethos and a ritual, all of which pointed to the one solemn end, which was the rite of passage out of childhood. Hence the Pony Club idea was enthusiastically taken up, as much by parents as by children, since it opened a door into the mysterious forms of membership that characterize rural life. The Club has been a powerful equalizing force, binding the children of farmers, labourers, tradesmen and teachers in a common discipline, and endowing them with the team spirit and competitive zeal that form the basis of a respect-filled social order.

Every summer, during the last week of July, we share in the excitement of 'Camp', as one or other of our protégées goes through her paces, earning badges, rosettes and status, and returning each day with new friends, new skills and new knowledge. Our protégées are the children of Romanian refugees: but Pony Club has fully acclimatized them to England; they understand the reticence, the formality, the uncomplaining tolerance and the need to be tough; most of all they understand and identify with the resolute independence of spirit that has been destroyed in their homeland but which still lives around here.

To reach the Camp you must take the horsebox through old farming country, where tractors and muckspreaders drive you off the road. It is an angry, masculine world, noisy and grim with the doom of livestock farming. Then dung-smells turn to hay-scents, the landscape tightens, and you bounce off the narrow lane into a sovereign matriarchal state. Mothers are directing traffic, stewarding arenas, marshalling children, judging competitions, running the tack shop, cooking lunches for the instructors, grooming horses, adjusting ties and jackets, thrusting sandwiches into pockets and sometimes refreshing themselves with a furtive gin and tonic in the polo tent.

They correspond to no familiar caricature of English country life: they do not bark or sniff; they are not dressed in green wellies or tweed skirts or old dungarees; they do not speak with toffee-nosed accents or warn the children not to fall orff their horse. They are quiet, businesslike, and eager; their faces glow with pride and a war-time sense of public duty. They are engaged in the magic of transition, the alchemical process that turns child to adult and adult to child. It is as much for them as for the children that this episode exists, and just as the children come away from a day's instruction with more serious airs, leading their ponies with proud and protective gestures, so do the mothers become sensibly younger, reliving their own first love of animals, falling into nonsensical horse-talk, and anxiously grooming their children for events that will test them both. Child and parent mingle their fortunes, in a rite of passage that takes one into the future, and the other into the past.

I was brought up on socialist resentment, fed with lies about the upper classes, and kept away from country life. In this matriarchal gathering I am the only man, sole representative of the seething suburbs, handing sandwiches to a child who is not even mine, and English only by adoption. Yet both of us are at home. This is not 'multicultural Britain' but unicultural England. And there before me is Christina, Greek Orthodox, francophone, and with dark Romanian features, climbing back with an authentic stiff upper lip onto the horse from which she just fell down.

4

Our Home

Settling down means bringing up, and both involve a commitment that is at odds with the modern world. An unsettled people soon loses the heart to reproduce itself, having no provision for its children save the whirlwind of chance. In our place, however, the marks of settlement are still discernible, scuffed away in places, trampled by global imprints but constantly and deliberately restored. Pylons march across our valley, the motorway hums its perpetuum mobile in the Vale of the White Horse, and the convoys of Hercules transports fly into Lyneham across the roof of our farm. But our little society, sad though it is, adjusts itself to the landscape, like a woman rearranging her tear-stained face in a mirror. And the conspiracy of the unborn against the living is here endorsed by everyone.

Continuity is the meaning of a country town, which keeps vigil over the surrounding landscape, feeds it from its arteries, and draws its surplus product to itself. That is why the vandalization of country towns is felt so much more keenly than the destruction of industrial cities, foci of experiment and change. And it has helped our people immeasurably that their two market towns of Malmesbury and Tetbury are still intact, even though both have lost their markets, while nearby Wootton Bassett has regained a farmers' market, set up beneath a Jacobean town hall.

Bassett Town Hall is raised on Tuscan columns above an open loggia, and stands in the centre of the town along the high street. It was restored to civic dignity in Thomas Hardy's day when, in the sheltered space behind its colonnade, corn and vegetables from the Marlborough Downs were exchanged against eggs and meat from the claylands. It was restored again in recent times, under the

directions of English Heritage, whose 'authentic' trusses and
beams in pale oak so offended local taste that the whole thing had
to be redone, in the black and white of Tudorbethan make-believe.
The result is a vivid proof that history is an invented thing, and
should be invented according to our modern needs and not according to the hidebound rules of scholarship. The Town Hall is the
past of Wootton Bassett, but the past spoken in the present tense,
so as to endorse the living market in the street below and to reas-
sure us, against the odds, that this is how it was and will be.

Wootton Bassett is separated from the encroaching nowhere-
zone of Swindon only by a thin strip of pasture. Its backstreets
have already been bulldozed, and its outskirts given over to
unsightly warehouses of windowless steel. Malmesbury lies further
from the source of aesthetic pollution, and is built on a hill above
a loop in the river Avon – a situation that defends it from exurban
development. Malmesbury's situation also lends itself to defence,
and explains why this town has had such an important place in our
history. Malmesbury is still bounded by fortified walls, and, where
these have crumbled, the orchards and parklands flow in among
the streets. In all directions save one, where Dyson's factory dominates the hillside, these streets lead into fields, and the outlying
buildings of stone make a conscious effort to broadcast Malmesbury's small-town dignity across the meadows.

Thanks to these meadows Malmesbury has managed to retain
its equilibrium, and to live in dialogue with the surrounding farmsteads. The town owes the meadows to its ancient charter, granted
in Saxon times, and to the 'Old Corporation', whose members, or
Commoners, are chosen from those who can claim direct descent
from the men who fought here under King Athelstan against the
Danes. The Old Corporation still exists, although its sovereignty
was destroyed, like so much else, by the Local Government Act
of 1888. The Commoners own patches of land around the town,
and, through their largely ceremonial presence, sustain the local
pride that has so far guaranteed the town's survival. They are a
modest version of Wagner's Guild of Mastersingers, tenaciously
maintaining customs whose rationale belongs inexplicably to a
place and its past.

The civic pride of Malmesbury can be witnessed in the Victorian
mansions that lie on the perimeter of the town. Built in local stone
by local craftsmen, acting without the impediment of an architect,

they form a fitting tribute to the wealth brought by local markets, and to the produce of the fields which lap their walls. One of them, given by its first owner to the town, now serves as the local hospital, and it is a model of what a hospital should be: serene, unhurried, a functioning part of the community, donor and recipient of charitable gifts. Sam Scruton was born in this building, and so too was his sister Lucy. For although Malmesbury hospital is without an anaesthetist and relies on the old arts of midwifery, the spiritual benefits fully compensate for the physical pain. Such, at least, was the line I took with Sophie, and to my astonishment she agreed with me.

First of those spiritual benefits is the great oak door, with its latch of cast iron, and its mock-Tudor arch of stone. This door creaks like the door of a church, and opens onto a quiet vestibule, from which you proceed past a roomful of cheerful old ladies to a wide newelled staircase and thence to the maternity ward on the upper floor. The rooms of the old house have been divided, but each has its share of neo-gothic mouldings, a stone arch or two, and corbel tables carved with oak leaves. Fix your eyes on these, Sophie tells me, and the pain is more bearable. Unlike the sterile surroundings of the modern hospital, they carry a message of affirmation. Like everything that our ancestors carved in stone, they are a bid for immortality, a statement that we like it here and are glad to have been born.

From the window you see what you see from so many windows in Malmesbury: meadows in which cows are grazing; clumps of willow, ash and hawthorn; a stone cottage or two; wooden fences and blackthorn hedges. On one side there is a neat kitchen garden with flowering marrows, sweetcorn and beans, on the other a paddock with two horses and a donkey. All this refreshes the spirit and raises the morale – not of the mother only, but also of the nurses, who move around these airy rooms as though at home there, bringing linen from panelled cupboards in armfuls and making their patients feel like guests.

And although all consciousness of one's surroundings vanishes in that last agonizing hour, when nothing avails save firm words and loving hands, the world that greets the reborn mother and her new-born child brings messages for both of them. It matters that an image of peace and permanence can be seen beyond the window; it matters that a quiet domestic space unfolds around the bed where they lie together. It matters that the child is born into a place, a community, and a culture, to take its place in the web of historical ties.

All those messages are conveyed by Malmesbury hospital, which also illustrates two propositions that seem to me to be both deep and true, and which are nevertheless denied by so many modern architects. First proposition: the architect Louis Sullivan's famous maxim – that 'form follows function' – is the opposite of the truth. Buildings should not be wedded to the purpose that first required them, but should rise above it, take delight in themselves, in their situation and in human life. They can then be adapted to any purpose we like. In a nutshell, function follows form: make a pleasing environment, and whatever we do in it will please. Hence Malmesbury hospital, which started life as a private house, is now an exemplary hospital, while Swindon's Princess Margaret Hospital, designed by a modern architect as a hospital and having no other conceivable purpose, is already abandoned and scheduled for demolition.

Second proposition: the aesthetic is no optional addition to our projects, but the very heart of them. Make a building look right and feel right, embellish it with mouldings and details, allow craftsmanship and tradition and the love of ornament, and the whole work is transfigured. The building becomes a companion, a participant in the human life contained in it. And when that life is new life, the building joins in the welcome.

What is true of Malmesbury Hospital is true too of Sunday Hill Farm. It is a simple cottage of stone, with upstairs and downstairs connected by a winding staircase in the corner. There is an attic, once used for storing grain, under a tiled roof that rests on beams of oak. The whole is supported by a massive chimney stack. Abutting the cottage on one side is a stone barn, with large doors in the long walls to allow the breezes to blow the chaff from the winnowed corn, and with an additional stable door for the horse. On the other side is a parlour, also of stone, added in the nineteenth century, but following the style of the original. The downstairs windows are embellished with arches of dressed stone, and a moulded string course runs the length of the facade, serving as a drip stone to protect the windows. The cottage and barn nestle at the foot of Sundey Hill, and are set back from the road by an orchard. The architectural historian Tim Mowle was charged with listing buildings of importance in our area. He was conscious, he tells us, of the economic damage done to farmers by the gratuitous listing of their farmsteads. For agricultural buildings must constantly adapt to the changing needs of the rural economy. As a result of Tim Mowle's approach, none of the buildings in our valley was listed, and therefore all are adaptable. But our house will surely never be demolished, for the simple reason that it has such a homely and settled aspect. It takes its form from the valley where it sits, and its substance from the stones beneath it. It is visibly at ease in its surroundings, and hence will survive every change, even the very great change that it has undergone in recent years, when the last attempt to make it work as a farm was abandoned, and an urban incomer lighted on it as a place to settle.

The fate of Sunday Hill Farm should be compared with that of Goddard Farm just down the road, recently abandoned by Bert, the tenant farmer. Bert's farm was one of many bought for next to nothing by Wiltshire County Council in its bid to revive the dairy industry in our part of the world. Everything that has happened to it since, however, illustrates some aspect of bureaucratic folly.

First the Council demolished the old farmhouse – a building of Cotswold stone, set back from the road amid outbuildings and a copse of trees, and with an aspect as settled and engaging as that of Sunday Hill Farm. Next the Council built a standard red-brick house by the road, and beside it a muddle of concrete sheds. These symbols of progress have dated as rapidly as the tower blocks of post-war London. Unlike the old farmhouse, which could have been converted to any rural use, these functionalist buildings are tied to the dying industry that required them, and their air of dereliction is only enhanced by the alien quality of their materials and by their mean refusal to belong.

The Council then built a hay barn next to the road, and in due course widened the road to give the whole thing a more industrial character. The effect was to increase the noise, the turmoil and the exposure of the farm, and to guarantee that the tenant would never feel properly at home there. Soon it was clear that Bert was farming not with the land but against it. His fields were a straggling mass of docks and rampant hedgerows, and the farmyard a heap of discarded machinery, household junk and shredded plastic. And when, three years ago, a passing arsonist jumped from his car and set the place alight – destroying a year's supply of hay and straw, and burning 24 calves to death – this was only to be expected.

The house survived the catastrophe, and the Council rebuilt the barn, only to discover that Bert had no intention to make use of it. The business was making a loss, the rent was no longer affordable and the arson attack had left him nervous and bitter. So the Council decided to sell, just at the time when no *bona fide* farmer could afford to buy. And having offered Bert enough money to induce him to renounce his tenancy – enough money, that is, to buy a bungalow in Wales – the Council put the farm up for auction in two lots, thus creating a potential planning catastrophe. By another stroke of bureaucratic madness, the planning department is a branch of the District Council, while the land belongs to the County Council. Hence the planners could do nothing to influence the Council's decision to divide the eyesore it had created and so make two eyesores in the place of one.

The auction took place in the King's Arms hotel in Malmesbury, and was attended by everyone. Farmers depend upon an intricate web of cooperation between neighbours, and every piece of land that is taken out of agricultural use, every cottage that is bought by a commuter, every barn that is converted to a suburban dream-home, is a threat to their future. The man who was seen to bid for Bert's farm with a small silent nod of the head bought the place as a whole. Moreover he was dressed in a green jumper and checked shirt, brown country shoes and a leather belt – reassuring signs which encouraged our farmers in the belief that cows will still be grazing there next year, that long-standing agreements will be upheld, that the docks will be sprayed.

Their hopes were not in vain. Vic, the second incomer to our valley, is a builder, whose wife runs a travel agency in Swindon. He has one ruling ambition for the farm that he purchased, which is to demolish the house by the roadway, and to rebuild the old farmstead as it was, so as to settle there with his family. Meanwhile the cows and the sheep are welcome, and farming goes on.

The desire to settle on a farm is not just a piece of modern nostalgia. For although it is true that, under the escalating pressure of urban life, people have increasingly sought to escape to green pastures and have painted those pastures in the imaginary colours of Eden, the sense that we are at home on the farm is a human universal, and records the pre-history of our species. That is why the farm has such an important place in children's literature. On his first birthday Sam Scruton was given an illustrated book for children, containing his first words of French. He didn't have a word of English and was behind-hand even with his Greek. Still, the gift was well-intentioned, and Sam was thrilled by it. And the page that he found most interesting was that devoted to *La Ferme*. Moreover it is the only page in the whole book that seems remotely to acknowledge the existence and validity of the old European society in which I grew up. There is a distinctively French-looking farmer; a house with a pitched roof and an old Dutch barn; chickens pecking at liberty in the farmyard; an old-fashioned red-coloured tractor exactly like ours; a cart-horse in the moss-covered stables, and a farmer's wife who seems actually to be engaged in housework. The horizon is bounded by a hedge – though, being French, it is unkempt and gappy. There are cows in the field and free-range pigs in the farmyard. And it is the man, not the woman, who is driving the tractor. In short, this page is an invocation of home, and an attempt to attach the deep yearnings of childhood to a real experience of settlement.

The rest of the book displays a world that is completely un-French, and completely detached from anything suggestive of a culture. The home contains not a single book ('livre' is a word that comes only towards the end, when we chance upon one of these relics in a cupboard at school). The furniture is modernist, plastic and international; the colour-schemes are garish and American; the people too are modernist, plastic and international. None of the old French characters is there: the plethoric priest, the starched old nun, the peasant with his *beret basque*, the *charcutier* with his paunch, *le facteur* and *le gendarme* with their quaint caps, Second Republic uniforms and neat moustaches – all have been censored out. The home has no musical instrument, no dining room or elegant furniture, and no clear provision for guests. It consists, in fact, entirely of gadgets: televisions, radios, mobile phones, Walkmans, computers, cameras, video recorders, CD players – with which the multicoloured and multicultural children play distractedly, receiving messages that are available everywhere and anywhere, and which are mostly made in America.

When we turn to the farm, however, we enter a place that was patently made in France. The landscape, the architecture, the clothes, the expressions, even the animals, have the unmistakeable look of things sheltered by village life, shaped by the language of Flaubert and by the faith of Paul Claudel. The cockerel is the *coq gaullois*, the cow reeks of *crème fraîche* and camembert, the pigs are manifestly on their way to becoming *boudins noirs* and *rillettes*. The man and woman have the quiet purposeful manner that comes from real work and natural piety, and their world is a gadget-free and labour-intensive realm of fulfilling industry, in which the good things in life are not carelessly squandered but slowly and patiently achieved.

Sam is not the only one-year-old to have noticed this. Indeed, there is scarcely a child who is not drawn to the farmyard, as the place about which it is most enjoyable to learn. The animals are of the first importance, of course, since children begin life with the genetic imprint of the hunter-gatherer, for whom nothing is more important than a familiarity with species. But children are also fascinated by the images of real labour, whose product is food and whose by-product culture. Even if the rural life were destroyed, therefore, we know that it will live on in children's books. It will live on because it preserves the deepest of our species-memories – the memory of the wild forest that was everywhere, and of the clearing that was ours.

But how do you bring up children in this clearing? Shortly after Sam was born I was invited by a national newspaper to describe his intended upbringing. Naturally, I assured the readers, he would be brought up on the classics, would be reading Greek like John Stuart Mill by the age of six and learning English the hard way, from a grammar written in French. He would study the viola as a salutary form of self-abasement, and be taught the virtues – courage, justice, prudence and temperance – in their Christian version, as forms of faith, hope and charity. And although Sam would probably not enjoy his childhood, he would emerge from it as someone agreeable to others whether or not happy in himself.

The article precipitated a storm of abuse from experts in child-rearing, educational gurus, feminists and assorted believers in progress. For several weeks we lived in dread of the social workers. If we could not answer their enquiries, we feared, Sam would be taken into care, denied all access to his parents, and given a normal diet of pop, television and takeaways. Our panic subsided, however, in tandem with the emendation of our plans. Sam showed little interest in English grammar, entirely neglected not only the piano but also the guitar and the viola, and confined his musical experiments to turning on the rhythm machine on my keyboard whenever he saw me working. His first word was 'prshi', which is Czech for 'it's raining', meaning on Sam's lips, however, anything from a helicopter to a dog turd. And his principal interest during his first two years was building. He spent his days with the men who were working on our extension, handing out trowels, heaving buckets, mixing his own version of cement, and occasionally using it to make plaster-casts of living chickens. Intellectually speaking he did not live up to my hopes or Sophie's fears, and yet his eager cooperative nature, his determination to be useful, and his narrow but real curiosity about the world of masculine labour endeared him to many hearts.

Like every anxious parent, I compare Sam with other boys, and I cannot help remarking how similar they are in one fundamental respect, which is that they all want to be men. Moreover, they all associate manliness with action, with the use of tools, with the making of something out of nothing, and with power and the machines that produce it. There are those who attribute this to culture: change the toys, the role models and the contexts, they say, and boys will dress up, play with dolls, coddle animals, and make little interiors where they can be snug as a bug in a rug. But there seems to be a great paucity of supporting evidence for such a view. Moreover, it flies in the face of what we know about sexual selection, about the evolution of humanity, and about the division of labour in hunter-gatherer societies. Hence, although we intended to bring Lucy up in the same harsh and improving regime that we proposed for Sam, we were fairly sure that she would not be seen, aged 12 months, with a trowel in her hand.

In the world described by Jane Austen men and women enjoyed separate spheres of action, the first public, the second private, the first involving influence without intimacy, the second intimacy which made little direct impact outside the home. Dress, manners, education, recreation and language all reinforced this division, with marriage as the great life-choice in which it culminated, and whose purpose it was.

Although there is no going back to that society, we do our children a disservice if we fail to acknowledge that their sexual nature sets them from the beginning on different paths. We should learn not to deny sex, but to idealize it – to set before our children an image of the good man, and the good woman, and to teach them to imitate what can be loved and admired. Even without the old division of roles, we can envisage alternative forms of role-playing which serve a comparable function – which rescue sex from animal appetite and make it the foundation of a lasting commitment.

Children, in their innocence, have an inkling of this. Sam with his trowel was idealizing himself, just as Lucy now idealizes herself as she tells stories to her dolls and tends their fictitious ailments. However, they are surrounded by those global and unsettling influences that seem determined to undermine all our ideals. Settling, for us, has meant a continual attempt to keep those influences at bay. And without a doubt the most troubling of them is television. Children are now brought up on it – indeed, according to the latest research, actually addicted to it.[21] Teachers are aware of the damage done by television to the brains, the morals and the attention-span of their pupils, and it is only doting parents who will now deny the obvious. Nevertheless, it seems a drastic decision to deprive a child of the messages and the images whereby all his little friends are socialized.

Ever since the birth of Sam, therefore, we have periodically debated whether or not we ought to acquire a telly, perhaps to be kept in a corner of the library with a cloth over it, or to be turned to the wall and secured with a padlock. Always, however, we have resisted the idea, knowing that if Sunday Hill Farm is an island of peace and stability this is because everything that happens here (apart from accidents and disasters) is our doing. Why give up what you do value, simply to be in touch with what you don't?

Still, that does not resolve the dilemma posed by our children. Should we, or should we not, deprive them of this thing which is shaping the future world – the world that they will inherit? Fortunately Sam solved the problem for us, and also helped us to overcome the cultural gap that separates us from our neighbours. As soon as he could fend for himself, Sam began to spend much of his time in other people's houses. As a result he introduced us to television, not as a fact but as a game. Instead of demanding that we acquire a telly-screen, he pretended from an early age that we already have one. It is located in the cast iron facade of the wood-burner, and its invisible knobs are attached to the panel above. Making use of the remote control from the CD player, Sam is able to summon his favourite images on to this screen, and also to introduce us to the culture of watching.

The first prerequisite of this culture is background noise. Sam tends to select *The Last Clarinet*, not because he follows the story but because Paul Englishby's felicitous music has an episodic character suitable to the little screen. Once the music is playing, Sam summons his parents to sit down. At our first attempt to play telly, we sat fairly upright on the sofa, as though to read, causing him to howl with dismay. 'That's not how you sit for telly,' he cried. 'You've got to lie down.' He demonstrated the TV slouch, as he had observed it in his sociological field-work, and commanded us to copy it. After a few attempts we got the hang of it, and were able to maintain the posture for several minutes, while staring at the wood-burner from vague and cloudy eyes.

'You need some food,' Sam went on, after judging our postures to be satisfactory. 'Maybe some bisnicks or a nana.' Returning from the kitchen with provisions, he thrust them into our hands and commanded us to watch as he fiddled with imaginary knobs and uttered electrical fizzes and crackles. Finally everything was ready for the great event, and, backing away slowly to his own chair, Sam settled in the required posture, pointed the remote control at the burner, and pressed one of the buttons.

'See there's a big digger,' he announced, 'and its coming down the road. Only the 'ment mixer's in the way. And they're going to have Tellytubby-toast, they're singing...'

After a minute or so of this, he handed me the remote control, suggesting that I select a programme. I pressed the button and continued the story of Henry and the water-dragon, at the point where we had left off. There on the screen is the dragon's pond, with the willows trailing their leaves in the water and the frogs gently croaking. Henry is coming up the hill to ask the dragon's help in his next adventure. You can see some of the horses, and the sheep that's stuck in the bush under the oak tree. Gradually I settle in to the narrative, while Sam gets up from time to time to adjust the brightness or turn down the noise.

For a while this game was a regular occurrence at Sunday Hill Farm, each of us taking it in turns to supply the story that would bring the burner to life. Everything that one hates about the telly – the sensationalism and vulgarity, the shapes, colours, sentiments and manners, the invitation to give up thinking, feeling, doing or imagining and to become a passive moron instead – all this was eliminated from our cast-iron screen. Our telly was the distillation of our own imaginative powers: not something that happens to us but another thing that we do. As far as Sam was concerned it also had a great advantage over the story-book, which is that it made us adopt the helpless posture that neutralized our claim to be in charge of things. In front of the telly we were all children together, and his programmes enjoyed equal status with ours.

Into our Eden, however, there creeps another and more insidious tempter. Decked out in malign primary colours, with humanoid faces and moronic jingles, the plastic monsters slip past our vigilance by whatever route they can – in the bags of visitors, in the post, or down the chimney at Christmas. Battery-driven buses which sing out the alphabet in mocking tones; diggers, dumper-trucks and tractors, all designed to cause maximum damage to the foot that steps on them; maddening plastic balls that play *Auld Lang Syne* or *Eine kleine Nachtmusik* until you throw them across the room, only to hear them break into 'Waltzing Matilda' as they hit the wall; or – my *bête noire* – a semi-collapsible steam engine in padded pink nylon, that looks as though designed by Jeff Koons, and which puffs and squirms obscenely as the child obsessively presses its switch. The tempter is the Toy, and it is a hydra-headed monster. For every toy that is culled, a hundred new ones spring up in place of it. By my calculations, each Western child must have received, by the age of reason (supposing he ever reaches it), 50 times his own weight of non-biodegradable, aesthetically poisonous and morally corrupting rubbish – all delivered with the best of intentions, by people who think that the child learns to understand the world by *owning* it. Seeing the Devil in this form tempts me to become a socialist.

Alberti, that *uomo universale* who thought long and hard about architecture, painting, philosophy, war, and just about everything else that mattered in Renaissance Italy, thought long and hard about childhood too. His conclusion, roughly speaking, was that childhood is a mistake. Moreover, it is a mistake that you don't have to make. With help from adults, you can fix your eyes from the earliest age on the world of rational beings, and steadily learn to imitate the virtues and loathe the vices that map out the moral landscape ahead. The one great obstacle to this, argued Alberti, is toys. By mocking and miniaturizing the world of adults, they also make it inaccessible. Toys lock the child into its earliest emotions, and jeopardize the possibility of ever relinquishing them.

Well, it is a possible view, and a tempting one. But perhaps this temptation too should be resisted. For there is a more genial side to toys, and that is their effect on the one who gives them. Toys are expressions of love and gratitude for a child, and also mild apologies to the Deity for not being quite so pleased with him as you ought to be. In sweetly forgiving mood, therefore, I accompanied Sophie to Malmesbury, to buy a toy for Lucy's second birthday: nothing large or loud or lugubrious, and certainly nothing in plastic. Just a small, soft, cuddly, degradable thing that would erode in the gentle stream of Lucy's kisses.

With that thought in mind, I stood outside the toy shop, awaiting Sophie's reappearance, and smiling benignly at the sunlit street. I maintained this – admittedly somewhat artificial – attitude until Sam, wriggling free of my inattentive grip, ran after his mother into the shop. His eyes alighted at once on a tractor – or rather on The Tractor, that is to say My Tractor, without which all prospect of a future life on this earth became instantly inconceivable. In vain did we remind him that the birthday in question was Lucy's; in vain did we recall the tractors already littering every inch of floorspace in his bedroom; in vain did we refer to the sin of selfishness and the unattractive sound of 'mine'. Soon there were tears, cries and wails of 'toy rage', and I began to apologize to the couple who keep the shop. 'Don't worry,' they said, 'most of them just lie on their back and scream until they're carried out.'

Later, having confirmed both Alberti's unfavourable view of toys, and his favourable view of corporal punishment, I began working myself up for another futile but therapeutic cull, cursing those Victorians who gave us the cult of childhood – Robert Louis Stevenson, for example, for whom 'toy' rhymes with 'boy' and 'joy'. Shakespeare gives us the true rhyme, the rhyme that puts a lid on the thing:

> *Who buys a minute's mirth to wail a week?*
> *Or sells eternity to get a toy?*
> *For one sweet grape who will the vine destroy?*

The answer is children, for whom that 'one sweet grape' will blot out all other goals unless we forbid it.

An addiction to fast food – which is really toy food, food made irresistible and addictive by its sweetened foretaste – is as serious a defect in modern children as an addiction to television, and it has the same adverse effects on social life. English and American children now enter adulthood without knowing how to cook. Even the art of boiling an egg is beyond them, and as for curing a ham, stuffing a sausage, or shaping a raised pork pie – forget it. This massive ignorance of what is, after all, the fundamental art of civilization, ensures that English-speaking people now have so little ability to survive outside cities that, wherever they go, they bring the city with them, plastering the countryside with takeaways and supermarkets, and scorning the local produce as an intolerable health-risk.

Even farmers are learning the supermarket habit. A troubling sight to a countryman is that of a farmer pausing mid-field in his tractor, and taking a Tesco sandwich from his pocket. Whatever happened to the bundle with its bread and cheese and its bottle of cider? When did you last hear a recipe on *The Archers*, or learn from *Farmer's Weekly* how to make neat's foot jelly or chitterlings of pork?

Old Mrs Bennet, who lives half a mile from here, has fought her own battle against cultural decline, believing that a house should be known by its taste as well as its furnishings. No olive oil in her recipes, no garlic or basil or lemongrass: lard, onions and strong perennial herbs like sage and rosemary create her immutable flavours. Of course, our wise rulers forbid her to sell her produce, but she is allowed to make gifts. One old farmer, now a widower, comes to her house each Sunday for his dinner. He is a cussid man who speaks to few of his neighbours. But from old Nancy Bennet he goes away with a smile on his face, restored as much by her quiet feminine competence as by the familiar taste of the England that he knew as a child. In exchange for little favours we obtain steak-and-kidney pies so beautifully blended that they taste better cold than hot (a test that no shop-bought pie has ever passed, in my experience, save those from the butcher in Cricklade).

Man ist was er isst – you are what you eat. Ludwig Feuerbach, to whom we owe this saying, made a habit of just missing the truth. It is not *what* you eat, but *how* you eat, that makes you: *man ist wie er isst*. The greatest divide in society is between people who sit down to meals with their families, and those who eat on the hoof. Farmers tend to belong to the first kind, while those who consume the farmers' products tend now to belong to the second.

Sam goes to play with the grandchildren at Mrs Bennet's farm, and sometimes we collect him at the end of the meal. Whatever the weather and however far from the farmhouse they are working, the Bennets will come home at midday to their dinner, and sit down at the family table. The meal is a hot one, exhibiting the staple diet of the English – roast meat, root vegetables, potatoes drowned in gravy, and afterwards a crumble or a pie. If the children are home they too will participate, as will the grandparents, siblings, nieces and nephews who accumulate in surprising quantities on farms.

These meals are remarkable for their silence, which is a peculiar contented, sociable silence, quite distinct from the silence of the lone commuter eating pizza on the train. It is laid like a cloth across the table, and provides a soft, clean background to the gentle sound of eating. Above this silence the members of the family communicate in wordless ways – helping the children to food, passing the ketchup, grunting and nodding when the pudding appears. This speechless conversation includes the new-born and the senile, and binds the whole family in a web of mutual dependence. Isolation is overcome, and anxiety stilled in the small including gestures of the table.

The silence of the dinner table is general, and also individual: each member has his own unique form of it, like a personal napkin retained from meal to meal. For long moments Mr Bennet communes familiarly with himself, his face lit from within by thoughts which have no equivalent in words, since they are the aftermath of action. His wife's silence is more preoccupied: the domestic calculations flit across her features, as she surveys the leftovers and plans the efficient use of them. Often she looks around her, since this is her sphere and the undone tasks are calling. Granddad too seems more completely himself, as he succumbs to the silence and prepares his large and friendly face for sleep. From his earliest years Sam was quite at home here, and often we would discover him on his high chair, pointing with his plastic spoon to the things he delighted to describe, but content in this place to leave them nameless.

For people of my generation such scenes were the central drama of family life. And food was the principal character in the drama – slow food, which made the passage from raw to cooked, from thing to stuff, in this very place where it was eaten. Food existed in three distinct forms: raw on the kitchen table, hot in the pan, and then divided and allotted on the plate before you. Each of these forms represented a kind of labour and a kind of sacrifice. And you knew that the three stages were mutually dependent, preparations for the final consummation, in which the Formica table, with its salt, pepper and ketchup, with its 'serviettes' in silver-plated rings and its blue china plates with kitschy rims of gold, became the sacrificial altar of the family.

Never for a moment did you doubt that this food, which was the focus of so much ritual and the fuel to so much shared emotion, was itself produced by families, whose job it was to till the soil and feed the flocks, and from whose labour those vegetables and joints emerged already marked by ownership. Ours was a suburban household of the *Ethel and Ernest* kind.[22] We hardly saw a farm. But the farm was always in the background of our thoughts. It was the original source from which we were, in the scheme of things, downstream. It was the archetype of home from which we had, through some primeval mistake, departed.

Down the road from my flat in London was a health food store which sold real wholemeal loaves, brought round from some central point of manufacture and sold at vast expence to those who needed their bread to taste of bread. That is where, in my unsettled urban days, I bought my bread, since a loaf, for me, must pass the meat test: does the bread of your sandwich out-taste the meat? The MacDonald bap is designed to fail this test. It is a gustatory softness, against which the burger stands out like a pile of dog-shit on a satin cushion. Real bread is never background but always foreground in the battle for attention. It is both a staple and a luxury, a means of survival, and a cause of celebration. It is a universal food and also a universal symbol of food and of the earth's kindness in providing it. Bread, like wine, is a sign of settlement, the first and most important result of the agricultural way of life. Hence its significance in the Old Testament, and its final apotheosis in the Christian Eucharist, in which bread becomes the sacramental presence of God Himself.

In the light of that you might suppose that real bread would be more readily available in the country than in the town. For months after coming to Sunday Hill Farm I searched for bread in our local high streets. I encountered several honest bakers, competing with each other to produce doughnuts, cottage loaves and granary bread, milky cakes and iced buns. But I found nothing to match the solid, walnut-coloured blocks that I had bought from the wan, vague creatures who ran the health food shop in Notting Hill Gate. I inquired with the neighbours: without exception they had graduated from their farmhouse product to the easy world of Mother's Pride. All paid lip-service to some dimly remembered grandmother, whose wholemeal loaves, with their yeasty taste and heady fragrance, had perfumed the farmhouse kitchen twice a week. But none had retained either the recipe or the desire to make use of it. The world had changed. Real bread had disappeared over the horizon, along with real everything else.

This fact adds one more difficulty to rural life. The choices are stark: go shopping twice a week, be content with stale bread, or bake your own. It soon became clear that only the last choice was rational. To go shopping in Malmesbury is to lose half a day; to eat stale bread in green pastures is to deny the spirit of the fields. Hence bread-making has become a twice-weekly ritual at Sunday Hill Farm, and one hugely enjoyed by the children, for whom there is nothing more delightful than to immerse their fingers in dough.

Our bread is simple, good-natured and rustic. It is an illustration of a principle that will concern me in the final chapter of this book, namely that rural life is an urban idea. Left to themselves rural customs disappear, siphoned away by city lights. They live again when urban people come like us in search of them. Hence the best rural bread is now an urban product. German, Spanish, French, Moroccan, Greek, Turkish, Russian and Czech – every locality is available in the city. Some of the secrets of their manufacture are revealed by Sam and Sam Clark in the Moro cookbook.[23] Sophie, who is related to Sam and Sam not by marriage but by divorce, believes that the Moro sourdough is a kind of celestial vision of the bread idea. However, Sam and Sam's sourdough takes two days to grow, and really needs La Nonna always present in the kitchen. The shape and texture recall the vanished rhythms of pony-trap and horse-plough. Real rural people couldn't possibly find time to make it. But the best of rural life goes on, nevertheless, exported from our cities as a dream.

Although real bread is made here only at Sunday Hill Farm, real vegetables are growing everywhere. My experience of 'webshalls', as Sam Scruton calls them, has never been very encouraging. After the war my parents, like many others, acquired an allot-

ment. Each evening, on coming home from work, my father would
thrust a fork into my hand and march me like some Siberian con-
vict to the place of tribulation. There we would dig in silence side
by side, for the sake of those vile tubers – turnip, swede, parsnip –
which, besides their very texture, so antipathetic to the taste-buds
of a child, stuck in my throat as the symbols of my daily torture,
and the conclusive proof of its futility.

My father had a genius for discovering vegetables that would
be both immensely hard to grow – requiring hours of digging, rak-
ing, trenching, sifting and manuring – and singularly unpalatable
when harvested: stringy, rust-flavoured greens, powdery broad-
beans with a taste of soap, carrots with wooden yellow cores, and
his masterpiece, discovered one day in a fit of inspired malice,
kohlrabi. When boiled to a pulp this central European cross
between cabbage and turnip manages to offer every combination
of taste and texture that is loathsome to a child. I cannot look at
one of these vegetables without recalling my father's thunderous
face on the first of those grim kohlrabi days, as we lifted the
snot-coloured slime from our plates and held it trembling before
us, he meanwhile denouncing our involuntary retching as a self-
evident and insulting pretence. He cursed the vile ingratitude of
children with all the force of the mad King Lear, insisting that not
a speck should remain on the plate if we were ever to get down
from the table.

Thirty years later I found myself in Olomouc, at a time when
there was nothing in the shops besides kohlrabi (*brukev*). It was
with great pride in my maturity that I bought some and ate it raw,
with a sprinkling of salt. I enjoyed the taste, the texture, and most
of all the internal victory over my childhood, symbolized in this
strange and strangely named vegetable, eaten in alarming circumstances and in a mysterious place. This experience was one part
of a long voyage of discovery, during the course of which I learned
that every one of those vegetables, to which my father had
assigned its own special role in his regime of vindictive punishment, exists in a benign version that brings life to the body and
peace to the soul.

I now have an additional reason to revise my views. The nearest vegetable shop, six miles away, is a supermarket, devoted to the
great goal of the modern economy, which is first to wrap the world
in plastic, and then to burn it up. Prudence, time, morality itself,

require that we grow vegetables of our own. Moreover, we are put to shame by the neighbours, whose thriving gardens, with the wigwams of beans and cornucopious cabbages, stand not behind but in front of their houses, symbols of order and objects of pride. Their spherical beetroots, conical carrots and oval potatoes win prizes at local shows, where the criteria of excellence are strictly Euclidean. There is a cheerful self-reliance in these regimented gardens which reminds me of a rally of boy scouts, all brushed up and ready for adventure.

Shortly after Lucy was born, not wishing to draw attention to my efforts, I dug a patch behind the house, hidden from view by black-boughed conifers. Discovering that the sun peeped in only rarely and the wind forever blew, I cut down the conifers and built a protecting wall in their stead. I rotovated, dug, and raked; I added wood ash, sharp sand, dung, more sand, until at last the glutinous clay soil could be crumbled between the fingers. And then I began to plant: lettuces, potatoes, spring onions, marrow seeds and a little patch of herbs. A few frail shoots appeared, and for a day or two I felt a surge of pride, envisaging a long summer of fresh vegetables, each evening lightened by the trip to the garden, and by the triumphant return with some unexpected delicacy that would justify my status as a husband and a father.

The rabbits ate the lettuce; the chickens dug up the onions; the herb garden was savaged by pigeons, and moles invaded the potato patch, undermining the shoots. A few courgettes appeared, but they were dry and shrivelled on account of some disease from which the marrow plant soon died, snapping off in my hands one day with a sigh, like some imprisoned soul in Dante. Meanwhile groundsel, thistles and dead nettles colonized the loosened soil, and before long it was necessary to rotovate from end to end, saying goodbye to the feeble residue of my spuds and cabbages.

I persevered however, and last year produced a number of lettuces, some herbs, and even an incipient beetroot or two. True, the lettuces, assessed at my going rate, cost about a hundred pounds each. However, they were clear proof, not only of virility, but also of my conquest of those childhood traumas. With what a proud heart I came back with the first lettuce, carefully washing it, annointing it, and placing it on the table for the family! And what did my son do when the delicacy reached his lips? He retched, and let his mouth hang open, so that the lettuce leaf slid down a thread of saliva on to the plate. *How sharper than a serpent's tooth it is/ To have a thankless child!*

As part of the vegetable cult, almost all the gardens in our neighbourhood have scarecrows, and considerable efforts are devoted to fitting them out. One of our local villages recently mounted a whole display of them – a scarecrow festival that lasted for all of two days. The verges were lined by these smartly turned-out visitors, each one addressing the passer-by from its pool of stillness like a visible sermon. Some had football heads with painted features, others wore hats over cloth and straw, others still had masks from the joke-shop or false noses with beard and moustache. Policemen, pop stars, prelates and politicians were all raised on their poles, to frown at the farmers and bewitch their young. And for two days it was as though the village – hitherto known only for the beautiful hedgerows that stitch field after field to its borders – had discovered its vocation. Each household had affirmed itself in competition with its neighbour, like the rival *contrade* of Siena at the Palio, and for two days this spot of earth rose to a higher plane, conscious of itself as a village and proud to be nowhere but here.

And then the weather changed. The hats drooped, the clothes sagged, and within hours the real defects of these scarecrows – their defects as scarecrows, that is – became apparent. With running paint and swollen masks, the paste and paper heads sopped up the rain. The jackets blew open, the sodden stomachs sank, the sticks swayed and scissored, and finally, in the middle of a dreadful thunderstorm, the whole lot were snatched up, disassembled and banished to the barns: proof that the people who fashioned these soluble things were not farmers after all, but the new generation of urban settlers.

Our scarecrow, however, still stands in the vegetable patch. He – we know it is a he since he wears my clothes – has weathered every storm, kept stationary vigil in the highest winds, has gone from wet to dry and dry to wet without any visible change to his physiognomy apart from a gradual detaching of the body from the head.

The reason is that he is stuffed not with clothes or pillows but with straw, from which the rain slides off. We call him Bertie, after Bertrand Russell. He has the same stature as his namesake, the same puny legs and pigeon breast, and the same large head balanced on a frail long neck like a chicken's. This head – a numnah, folded up and clipped with a clothes peg, which serves as Bertie's nose – has the same vaguely prophetic expression as the philosopher, and Bertie holds himself erect, in the posture of one arrested in thought, with arms hanging slightly forward, poised between rising and falling – rising to illustrate a maxim or falling to punctuate a doubt. And often, in the light of the setting sun, when the long strands of white string that form his hair catch the low light and glow romantically, I recall the great philosopher on television, his electric hair shining around his leonine features, his mellifluous voice emerging as though by ventriloquy from lips that never seemed to move.

Russell was a great fighter of pointless battles, from pacifism during the First World War to nuclear disarmament after the Second. Bertie is similar. The crows, magpies, pigeons and blackbirds that ransacked our garden before his advent have continued their sorties with undiminished vigour under Bertie's nose. And I suppose this is what is most appealing about scarecrows – their very human attachment to what is essentially a lost cause. I have never come across a crow or magpie that paid the slightest respect to a scarecrow, and when I see one of these all-too-human figures crucified amid the growing crops, I wonder at the farmer who put him there and who must surely have been moved by some religious instinct. The English scarecrow is like the Central European Calvary – an icon of the supernatural, and an invocation of God's grace. In his *ecce homo* stance in open fields he becomes a symbol of our human helplessness, and of our determination nevertheless to resist our fate.

Hence Barbara Euphan Todd's stories of Worzel Gummidge, whose name spells out in Anglo-Saxon syllables that this scarecrow is the deeper meaning of the English landscape. Gummidge first appeared in 1936, part of the great spiritual upheaval that caused the English to search for their soul in the soil. He belongs with H. J. Massingham, A. G. Street and the original Archers. His mission is to defend the family farm against the modern world. Hence his magical powers, for nothing short of the supernatural can protect either the family or the farm from the global entropy. Worzel Gummidge keeps vigil over the old society and the old economy, a futile but much-loved martyr to the crows.

Bertie is still holding out at the bottom of our garden, and he too is a protector of the family farm, standing unmoved amid the marauding magpies, uniting my clothes and Sophie's horse-tack in a visual epitome of our marriage. Bertrand Russell wrote frivolous things about marriage, and had a lamentable tendency to express his undying love for one woman just when sliding into bed with the next. Wittgenstein said of him that his books should be divided into two kinds: those on logic, mathematics and formal philosophy, which should be bound in blue and which people should be compelled to read. And those on politics, morals and public life, which should be bound in red and forbidden. I like to think that Wittgenstein would have been happier with Russell's namesake. Bertie may have made no contribution to formal logic; but there he is at the bottom of our garden, still standing for eternal values in a world of reckless change.

There are two sure ways to wean children away from toys. One is through ponies and the Pony Club. The other is through magic. The cheap tricks of the cartoon film and telly screen accomplish every kind of metamorphosis, but only at an impassable distance that leaves the child's sense of wonder uncommitted and fatigued. Real magic means real people, real animals, and feats that elicit gasps of amazement from the crowd.

Two years ago, passing Martin's farm at the top of our hill, I came across a sight which is now so rare that I briefly thought I might have imagined it, in one of those daydreams which punctuate my walks. There in the roadside pasture is a circus. Not a big top, with caged animals, Disneyfied amusements and humming generators, but a tiny, atomic circus, almost a toy: as though someone has tried to fly a tent across the Atlantic, and has now fluttered down among our cows and horses.

Around the tent is a cluster of roadsters' wagons, and a hand-worked merry-go-round, painted in that beautiful sober maroon that you see on Parisian *portes-cochères*. The largest wagon bears the inscription *Gifford's Circus, established 2000*, but the date is surely ironic, since the classical lettering is embellished with rococo scrolls in gold, bearing the unmistakable imprint of the *commedia dell'arte* – that classical art-form which gave birth to the romantic way of life. From Watteau to Picasso, from Goethe to Bruno Schulz, this way of life has been celebrated in our art as a symbol of man's pilgrimage through loneliness, and of the accidental character of grief and joy. But surely nobody believes in it today? Anyway, what is a circus doing in Martin's field, and why is it so elegant and unencumbered, like a circus of the mind?

I go to enquire: yes, there are performances. And as I study the programme all is suddenly made clear to me. The creators of this circus are Toti Gifford and his wife Nell Stroud – our own Nell Stroud, who lived here before her mother's accident, who came to me for advice when going up to Oxford, and who has had one immovable ambition since a tiny girl, which is to join a circus – a real circus, in which art and life are woven together in a vision of innocent joy.

The next evening we buy tickets and join the crowd in Martin's field: it is a capacity audience, and 300 faces, most of them familiar, press against the tiny ring. Children, exhilarated from the merry-go-round, squirm on the laps of their parents, clapping their hands in anticipation. Taciturn farmers give short barks of experimental laughter. There is an old lady in a wheelchair, a group of toughs in baseball caps, local landowners and assorted merchants from Minety. People shout greetings as though they have not spoken for years and George, who reads the lesson on Sunday and fills the church with his booming voice, makes a *basso continuo* beneath the general hubbub. A clown in Charlie Chaplin dress amplifies the flow of giggles, moving among the crowd with the magic aura of a figment, visiting us from a realm which we could never enter. And then there is a roll on the drums and we all fall silent.

The curtains fly apart, and into the arena, with one beautiful bound, comes a palamino pony, its long silver mane shaking down to its hocks as it kneels before us, its nostrils distended in a theatrical snort. And there on top of it is Nell, her bright eyes – smiling everywhere but looking nowhere – transforming the ring into an imaginary space, a space of dreams and miracles. The pony dances in time to the music, and all the children hold their breath in wonder, seeing for the first time this animal which they pass every day in the fields. *Haute-école*, as it is called, is not a matter of training a horse to do clever tricks; it is a way of making the horse become what it could never become without the human emotion that masters it – a creature of the imagination, a mythological being whose essence lies not in flesh but in stories.

A pantomime horse comes to reinforce the message: here before us is the world that we knew as children, miraculously restored to us. The acrobats who hang from the copolla are no longer hampered by gravity, since they are not bodies but ideas. Baby Lucy watching them spontaneously imitates their movements, holding her breath in sympathy and seeming almost to rise towards them from her seat, lifted into the world of dreams. And through everything there runs the primeval drama, of the unattainable beauty who swings among the ropes above us, and the clown who strives fruitlessly to reach her, conveying through his greasepaint smile the loss that is yours and mine and everyone's, and for which there is no remedy save laughter.

Circuses like Nell's have a profound moral purpose, which is to make us re-imagine our own condition, first by showing us in proximity to the animals, mastering and completing them, second by idealizing the human body. Jugglers, acrobats, dancers, contortionists and trapeze artists – all emerge from the envelope of flesh, to become things of the mind. They are a hymn of praise to consciousness and to its power to remake reality. And behind each of them is that secret, wandering life that is rooted nowhere in the physical world.

But circuses have another deep appeal, which is that of innocence. It is entrancing to stand before this magic space, where there is nothing more explicit than the frilly knickers of a can-can, and where love and delight are returned to their rightful place in the scheme of things.

In *Josser*, the gripping tale of her apprenticeship,[24] Nell describes the tragic loss of her mother, who was thrown from her horse, to live thereafter as a vegetable. All of us felt that loss, since Charlotte Stroud was a life-force, mother to the entire community, who inspired us to become what we are. Through her circus Nell has rescued that life-force from extinction, and re-shaped it in imaginative form. And visiting us, she brought her mother's spirit home.

That such innocent events can occur in our fields is testimony to the trust that prevails between neighbours. Nevertheless, we are near the motorway, and down the motorway comes trouble. Our local philosopher, who signed himself 'Thomas Hobbes of Malmesbury', owes many of his great insights to the experience of civil war. Take away common obedience, he argued, and the result is not liberty but a 'state of nature', in which life is 'solitary, poor, nasty, brutish and short'. The remedy is to join in a social contract, by which we all surrender to a single sovereign, and confer on that sovereign the powers sufficient to govern us. No society can survive if it does not establish and defend such a common obedience, and divided societies are societies on the brink of destruction.

Unpunished crime is a threat to the social contract. Crime is a unilateral return to the state of nature, punishment the collective attempt to escape from it. In rural districts, where you are over-exposed to intruders and unprotected by the police – whose strategy is to arrive when the danger is past – crime goes largely unpunished. And unpunished crime sends the message that the sovereign is powerless, so that it is every man for himself.

This was the message understood by Tony Martin. Seeing his farm unprotected from people who exultantly displayed their contempt for him, he decided to fight back. And it was only when presented with this normally law-abiding, easily arrestable citizen that the forces of law and order bestirred themselves. Tony Martin was charged with murder, found guilty and condemned. Punishment, far from restoring the social contract, tore another hole in it. And, although Tony Martin's sentence was eventually reduced, it was through an unjust and humiliating demolition of his character, rather than a vindication of his act, so ensuring that the contract remains unrepaired.

Around Malmesbury crime, and the response to it, seldom has such a drastic and tragic air. Of course there was the notorious case of Thomas Hobbes's father, rector of Brokenborough, who killed one of his parishioners on his doorstep, perhaps by way of illustrating to young Thomas what the state of nature really means. But since those times things have gone rather quiet. A ram-raid on the chemist's, vandalism of the market cross, acts of rustic indecency and a riotous punch-up in a pub – last week's score illustrates our general sleepiness. And, with the departure of our arsonist, we in the claylands go for long periods with no crime at all.

Our most recent invasion, however, illustrates the character of rural crime. Entering a nearby village, the thieves stole bicycles from a farm and cycled over to our crossroads, where Freddy lives alone in his rented cottage. Freddy is confined to a wheelchair; but his son runs a haulage business from the yard behind the cottage, and keeps his lorry there. Freddy was asleep when the criminals arrived, dozing in his wheelchair with a shotgun at his side. He had drawn from the case of *R v Martin* the opposite lesson to that intended. You are on your own, he concluded, so make sure you're armed. Fortunately he did not wake up until his son's lorry was well out of the yard and heading down the narrow lane to Malmesbury.

There, however, the thieves encountered a hitch, in the form of James, who was driving his herd of Friesians along the road. James's cows have an exasperating but creative way of obstructing the flow of traffic, moving quickly into any gaps that might open, ambling along in front of you and serenely ignoring the gate to their field. Confronted with this impediment the thieves abandoned the lorry and made off into a field of maize. The police, by now alerted, surrounded the field and put it under surveillance.

Even with the aid of radios, cars and helicopters, however, human beings are unequal to the task of locating their fellows in such a dense sea of vegetation, where movement at the bottom barely rustles the top. For several hours the police guarded and patrolled the field. An offer of two Alsatians was politely refused, and when James started up his combine harvester this too was taken as a joke. Meanwhile the thieves slipped past the cordon into another village, where they discovered a tip-up truck and made off with it. Soon they were out of the district, and the police back in the station, filling out forms.

Not a very alarming episode perhaps. But suppose Freddy had woken to confront threatening intruders, and with no defence besides his shotgun? 'Taking the law into your own hands' was rightly condemned, when there were more effective and more impartial hands to summon. But the police are too busy on the highways to visit the by-ways. The recent case of a farmer who chased a burglar in his car across two county boundaries, while telephoning in vain for the police on his mobile, fully illustrates the principle established in *R v Martin*. The police ignored the burglar, and arrested the farmer for driving while using a mobile phone.

Crime is not the only reminder of the fragility of human life. Death resides in the country more outspokenly than in town: our bids for permanence are here more rapidly corroded, and the wild animals show that life and death are inseparable, yoked together till the end of time. Hence no child brought up in the country can be shielded from the truth about mortality. For the first two years of his outdoor life Sam Scruton confronted death without emotion. Rats and crows needed 'banging', which Roddy did with his gun, and Sam studied this fact with impartial curiosity. The living rat was superseded by the dead rat; and this change in the scheme of things was, for Sam, simply another proof of Roddy's competence, no different from the brick-laying, log-cutting and tractor-driving which established Roddy as the supreme authority in Sam's world. Later, however, Sam began to understand that death is the loss of something, and that the loss is irrevocable.

The process began with a chicken – a Suffolk white, which we had hatched ourselves, and which was just beginning to lay. Its birth, chick-hood and dawning maturity had been watched by Sam with growing fascination: here was a young creature making a niche for itself in the life of the farm just as he was, acquiring the arts of survival and becoming at one with its surroundings. Sam and the chicken were on cordial terms, and would greet each other with clucks when they passed in the farmyard.

During the period of Foot and Mouth disease, when there was no hunting, the foxes acquired the habit of patrolling the farmyard in full daylight; and the first victim was Sam's chicken, which disappeared up the hillside in Reynard's jaws, leaving a trail of white feathers on the grass. Sam greeted the news in silence, thought for a moment, and then asked when the chicken would come back. It took some time for him to absorb the meaning of 'never'; and his first response was to say that we must catch that fox and bang him – adding that it might first be advisable to chop off his tail. For a week or so thereafter Sam would ask anxiously about the criminal, warning us that he was prowling in the yard, or urging us to lock up the chickens just in case. Once, catching sight of the fox on the hillside, where he was digging for worms, Sam gave a piercing cry of fear, and this fear for a while took up residence inside him, surfacing in strange evocations of the big black fox-tummy from which the luckless chicken would never return.

Then Mervyn left a brace of pheasants at the door. At first Sam understood that these were just like any other pheasants, only dead, and when he asked who had 'deaded' them and was told that it was Mervyn he seemed quite satisfied that their rigid appearance lay in the nature of things. Ten days later, however, he watched me plucking one of the birds, and his senses were besieged by the sights and smells of putrefaction. It again dawned on him that he was witnessing a final and irrevocable extinction. Several times he asked whether this bird had been particularly naughty, that it should have met the same fate as a rat.

Then, when Malcolm the gamekeeper left a brace of mallards in the porch, Sam's gorge briefly rose in rebellion. He stroked their sleek shiny feathers, and tried in vain to open their eyes. He declared that it was a naughty man who had done this thing, and that we should punish him, just as we should punish the fox. Death was an intrusion into the Eden of Sam's consciousness – an intrusion that his parents had culpably failed to prevent. Regretting the mallards he was rehearsing for the first time the 'work of mourning', as Freud called it, which alas he will one day need.

Ours is a pleasure-seeking, death-denying culture. We lack the religious perspective that teaches us to accept our mortality as a spiritual good, and we put our faith not in God but in doctors. Hence we cling to life by whatever means, and by doing so make the mistake of dying too late, unmourned and unregretted. There are few prospects more bleak than that of the future promised by modern medicine, in which unloved geriatrics will perpetuate themselves with the spare parts robbed from human embryos. Country life teaches another doctrine, which is that death is the price paid for life and that it is a price worth paying, if it is paid on time.

Our home is safe, quiet and comfortable. From time to time, however, I am troubled by a lack. Having been brought up since the war I take prosperity for granted. But I also sense that something in human nature – something necessary for happiness – is threatened by our supremely cushioned existence. I experiment with descriptions of this missing thing: risk, privation, struggle, guilt, religion. But while we don't have enough of any of those things, none of them explains, through its absence, the sense that we are not living rightly. Last winter, however, the Scrutons discovered the truth: what we need is disaster.

It happened in the middle of the night. A Schubert song was sounding in my dream, in an orchestral version for which I was in some way responsible. I was sitting in the empty auditorium during the rehearsal, bothered by the percussion part. Where the texture needed muted tremolandos on the timpani there was an irregular percussive crack, which fell across the music like a whip, scarring the tender melody. I listened in horror, wondering how I could have made such a mistake. Every attempt to re-dream the dream had the same result, with the cracking sound erupting ever more frequently from the percussion section.

And then I remembered: it was the sound of exploding asbestos – the sound I had heard three years ago, when Bert's barn was set on fire. I was instantly awake and out of bed, staring from the window at the spark-spangled flames as they burst through the roof of the stables and leapt across the night. I shouted to Sophie, ran down to the door and over the frozen driveway, my bare feet insensible to the ice-glazed pebbles.

The stables were pitch dark, the lights all fused. We could see no horses: only shifting outlines in the smoke. But their fear was tangible, and the acrid fumes that curled around us were like the reaching hands of death. As yet the fire had not breached the door of the tack-room. It roared in its cage like an angry dragon, testing each crack with tongues of flame. To get to the horses we had to crawl beneath the smoke and reach up to the bolts of their stable doors. Somehow or other, with smarting eyes and convulsing lungs, we managed it, and emerged at last from the corridor into the yard. The horses were saved!

Except that no horse had followed us down the corridor. Retracing my steps I saw that each was trying to hide in the corner of its box, kicking at the smoke in a vain attempt to defeat it. I got in behind Sam the horse and pushed with all my strength against his brisket. Suddenly, swinging on his heels, he rushed into the corridor. With the imitative instinct of herds, the others followed. And I ran behind them, half blinded and gasping for breath.

But Kitty was not in the yard. Peering through the smoke I saw her kicking and rearing, as Sophie and Christina tried in vain to turn her head from the far corner of the stable. The head-collars were ablaze in the tackroom, but I remembered a rope coiled in the back of the tractor, and set off at a run for the barn. It was a minute before I found it, another minute before I had made my way back.

'It's OK, we led her with a hay-net,' said Sophie, who came staggering, faint and pale, from the stables. The flames roared in the tack-room, filling the window with an orange glare, and dancing high above the exploding roof-sheets. Five years of patient work was vaporising before us, and we watched it happen in silence. And then, unaccountably and all at once, a great surge of happiness came over us. It was a beautiful night, with the milky way clearly visible. Orion's belt gleamed majestically, indifferent to our petty troubles. A shooting star pencilled the zodiac, heading into sudden darkness, and the frosty pasture shone faintly in the starlight. We could just make out the forms of the horses, where they stood in the distant corner of the field. And then the blue light of the fire-engine appeared on the far horizon, and we knew that the stables too were saved.

Our fire brigade consists largely of part-timers and volunteers. Many of them have known each other since school; most were born in these parts and regard their work as a celebration of their way of life, a constantly renewable carnival, in which a shared history is saved in the nick of time from the flames. They arrive in a cheerful bundle, eager not just to put out the fire in the stables but also to soothe the fire in the heart. One of them is a housewife, who contributes her services for free; another runs a paint shop in the town. Being among them was like coming home from an ordeal, talking failure into another kind of triumph.

In the morning everything was newly delightful, like the world of a convalescent. The animals were grazing in their rugs, their charred saddlery stacked against the stables, emblem of death defeated. Neighbours were arriving with gifts of kindness and loans of tack. We were beginning again: things, animals and people were all on our side. We had lost our possessions; but we had regained a life.

5

Our Place

As winter approaches the fields reveal their shapes, the trees stand bare and tenacious on the hilltops; hares are alert and exposed in the grass; rabbits bob along the ditches and the fox saunters from covert to covert. These fields, you remember, have names, each redolent of a history and of the people who created it. The slope before my window is Sundey Hill – presumably sundered from the great estate of Malmesbury Abbey, a 'sundry' parcel of once useless land. The field below is 'Cuckold's corner', that above it 'Hanging hill' – the local lore being that it was here that miscreants were made to pay the ultimate price of their sins, some of them no doubt committed in Cuckold's corner. By the house is 'Wake's piece', and next to it is 'Dollakers' – presumably Doll's acre, on which, until recently, stood a stone cottage, reduced now to a few half-covered flagstones in the grass. This is our 'somewhere', the unsuspected goal of many wanderings, and as it bares itself for inspection I have the distinct impression that it looks back at me from a hundred eyes – the eyes of those who have lived and worked on this hillside, and who left their marks on the land: hedgerows, ditches, coppices, an overgrown orchard, two carp-ponds, and a green lane along the eastern boundary.

Green lanes are often places of great beauty, with ancient hedgerows and ditches, and untilled verges where wildflowers grow. They were the rights of way of rural England – unpaved, all but impassable in winter, but repairing themselves in spring, and linking the farms whose boundaries they drew. They are the filaments of an enduring web, and our lane is marked on the oldest maps of our district.

The lanes were never easy going. But they had an innate power of regeneration, under the influence of winter rainfall and the growth of spring-time grass. Our own green lane, which is now a bridleway, is too soft and narrow for the normal cross-country vehicle, and so has retained its character, as a living and self-healing thing. And in the winter it takes on a beautiful remoteness. Its soggy surface, bordered by blackthorn hedges where the red beads of bryony linger into the new year, acquires a faint silver sheen, and the sparse winter light lies in flakes on the waterlogged ruts, as though scattered there.

It is in the winter that such places provide their most lasting refreshment to the eye. For life has retreated, leaving its many colours half-hidden but perceivable, and the landscape is filled with a subtle counterpoint that could never be captured in a photograph. The lesson so patiently taught by Corot, Turner and Cézanne – that no natural object is truly monochrome, and that even in the blackest thicket can be discovered all the colours of the palette – is repeated by winter. And that is why there is no better time to visit the country, to walk or ride in the fields, and to take the chance of the weather for the sake of the eyes.

Indeed, the worse the weather, the more refreshing the effect. Green dissolves in water, loses its sickly surfeit, and allows the residual notes of autumn to appear through the storm. Driving rain and wind-tormented branches fill the air with spangled flakes of red and brown. The bare trunk of an ageing hawthorn, deprived of its green mantle and its distracting gift of berries, comes suddenly alive, its bark streaked with vermilion, folded into itself and breaking away to reveal long stretches of polished pewter. The mottled gold of the weeping willow, the deep crimson hue of the dogwood, the pallid cinnamon of the field maple, the many tobacco-leaf, rust-coloured and auburn highlights in the bark of an ash: all these are a source of delight, once you begin to notice them. The last ogee leaves of hazel, saffron yellow at the edges, but shading into green, recall the colours of the nut itself, while here and there in the hedgerows the vermilion rosehips and the last purple sloes give a poignant farewell to the life that produced them, like jewels in an old lady's hair.

It is an interesting exercise to stare into a dark, denuded hedgerow and count the colours. Every shade of red and blue, from salmon pink to scarlet, and from deepest indigo to pale forget-me-not, is lurking there, recuperating from the light of summer. And as you watch these hues glimmer like embers you come to understand some of the mystery of colour: how red excludes green, and yellow blue; how white is somehow not a colour at all, and the metal shades are like glosses in which colours are trapped and made invisible. These strange phenomena are not explained by the physics of light – a fact that Goethe noticed, and which led him to compose his great treatise on colour. They are not facts about things, but about *us seeing things.* Pondering them we are also pondering the mystery of consciousness. How is it that the world not only *is*, but also *seems*? Why was it not sufficient for the world to *be*?

The daily encounter with colour, in its ever-mutating, ever-striving natural form, is one of the joys of rural life. And this joy is recorded in country clothes – in the dusky green of woollens, in the understated chromaticism of tweeds, and in the subdued harmony of 'rat-catcher', in which every shade of blue and brown is somehow melted into a quiet amethyst. I even believe that real colour, because it is a kind of dialogue between the eye and what it sees, is part of what attaches our neighbours to the land, and rewards them, in these times of hardship and uncertainty, with the sense that life, after all, is worth it. But I also know that, when I stride through the winter dusk on Christmas day, they are snuggled up before the telly.

Of the changes that usher in the winter, none is more sudden or violent than the change in Iris pond. Almost overnight the warm brown sludge that has been thickening, fermenting and breeding for half a year is replaced by a brimming bowl of steel-grey water, hastening through on its way to the brook. The dancing boatmen have gone from the surface and the dragonflies are no longer pinned to the air; the water lilies have drowned, the fish have retreated to the bottom, and the heron has migrated. A few moorhens pick at the banks, but they too leave after a despondent week or two. Soon the trees are bare, and the other pond higher up the hill begins to overflow into the ditches, bringing down the frothy remnants of summer: leaves, twigs, acorns, and the pellets of owls.

This sudden change is a sign that the grass and trees have ceased to take in nutrients, so that the rain flows quickly into the hollows, and thence to the pond. Until next summer the water will remain a uniform metallic grey, gushing from the ditch above and into the ditch below with a noise like a hydroelectric dam. Iris pond will no longer be a self-contained and self-sustaining system, but a channel through which the irresistible winter flows. It will undergo in miniature the fate of our rural economy, as outside forces sweep away the fecund corners of contentment, and propel us on to the jostling global highway.

Hence ponds are a salutary object of study for those who wish to understand the world's predicament. Ponds stand still in summer, and their stillness ferments into life. You too become still beside a pond, drawn into its secret brooding, sensing without seeing the creatures that breed in its depths.

> *There are a sort of men whose visages*
> *Do cream and mantle like a standing pond,*
> *And do a wilful stillness entertain...*

What Shakespeare captures in the phrase 'cream and mantle' is something that only he could have put so luminously – the strange way in which the surface of a pond both hides and reveals the life beneath it, translating mysterious depths into a play of light and shade and texture. There are heat-logged days in summer when the surface of Iris pond resembles the 'great grey-green greasy Limpopo river', when the floating sticks are like somnolent crocodiles cushioned in their bubbles, when the damsel flies hang motionless over the water and the lilies stare at the sun. A concentrated, yeasty life seems to be growing out of sight, like an egg beneath a broody chicken.

Then, at sunset, this life is suddenly put on display. Dragonflies emerge from the banks, zig-zagging after gnats and midges; fish pop from the water, their orange mouths closing on long-legged flies; swallows swoop down to skim the surface, ducks glide in from nowhere and waddle on the muddy island, and a light breeze magically changes the water from an opaque soup of Rembrandt flesh-tints to a shimmering grey-blue like the glades of Corot. Such changes do not interrupt the stillness. They are shifting colours on a face, signs of the changing mood of a changeless personality. Ponds are places which look up at you, and you stand beside them in a kind of dialogue. They provide an eloquent example of something that people are missing and seeking in the modern world – namely, a *personal* relation to a *place*.

Ponds have personality because they are homes – self-sustaining habitats, abounding in renewable life. Some of the vegetation around Iris pond was planted there: guelder-roses, wayfarer shrubs, privet and cherry trees. But most is a natural product of the damp and the stillness: gypsy-wort, horsemint, reed mace, yellow iris, water crowfoot and the algae on which the pond life feeds. There are voles, frogs, newts, water snails and toads, as well as the beetles, rotifers and water mites essential to the aquatic food chain. Ducks – mallard and widgeon – have settled and bred, alongside the ubiquitous moorhens and every now and then a pair of Canada geese. Even the heron, unwelcome though he is, forms part of the renewable order, and only the cormorants, seafaring plunderers with the bedraggled look and the fierce mentality of Vikings, pose a threat to the equilibrium.

Romantic poets and composers spent many hours in the vicinity of streams and rivers, listening to the unending flow of clear water, as it rang the changes over polished stones. But, unless tied to a personal drama, as in Schubert's *Die Schöne Müllerin*, rivers suggest a false view of our condition. They are images of inexhaustible wealth, of external forces endlessly passing through, bringing with them freshness and energy. Tennyson's brook declares that

... men may come and men may go,
But I go on for ever.

But that is self-evident nonsense: just ask yourself what happened to the streams of ancient Greece. Life is a fragile system of mutually dependent elements, each of them minutely sensitive to change, generating energy in murky corners where mutually hostile creatures live in symbiotic aggression. To meditate by a stream is to fortify the romantic illusion of nature, as a benign force that outlives our mortal skills. To meditate by a pond is to be aware that nature is fragile, murky and mysterious, organically dependent upon human choice.

I am inspired to similar thoughts, too, when I contemplate a muck-heap. From our bedroom window we see green fields and hedgerows; in front of them a copse of young trees and nearer still our muck-heap. In the cold light of a winter dawn, when frost binds the landscape and no birds sing, when life has shrunk to a barely audible flutter in the hedgerows and the ditches are stopped with ice, the muck-heap takes on a special beauty – the beauty of a living, breathing, domesticated thing. A tranquil cloud of steam curls upwards from its top, softening the view of distant pasture, and each day as it decomposes the waste becomes warmer and tighter. The heap is a reminder of rebirth and fertility. For this cake of rotting waste is not waste at all: it is the ointment that heals the battered landscape.

Nor is it really a heap. In fact it is a work of careful architecture. It has a step in front and squared corners; its sides have been beaten into verticals with a hay fork, and its top has been trampled down and levelled. That is what must be done, not only to save space, but to ensure that the dung and straw compact and ferment as they should. To make the best muck you must keep horses on straw through the winter, cleaning out the stables each morning, and packing the contents so that they rot down into a greyish mattress. But that is only the first stage. You must then transfer the heap to the cow shed and spread it on the floor, where it forms a warm bed for the winter, and receives the more fluid droppings of creatures who chew and drink all day. You clean out the barn in the spring and leave the contents to rot through the summer. It will need at least six months before you can spread it, and the longer you leave it the more friable and soil-like it becomes. After two years it is alive with bright red worms, has the rich shiny blackness of a Christmas pudding, and smells of hessian and treacle.

Plants take nutrients from the soil and these nutrients must be replaced if the land is to remain fertile. Modern agribusiness involves a massive injection of nitrogen every year, in the form of industrially-produced nitrates that are scattered over the land and washed in by the rain. The calories needed to produce these chemicals exceed by many times the calories delivered by the crops that absorb them. Nitrate-enhanced soil also needs to be sprayed with selective herbicides and pesticides if the goal is to be achieved – the goal being fields which can be harvested automatically, by the contracter with his vast machine.

The alternative is the muck-heap, which adds nitrogen, top-soil and the worms that help in its regeneration. This method of renewal, advocated with almost religious zeal by A. G. Street, the Wiltshire farmer who made farming into a national icon through his wartime programmes for the BBC, does not restore the land only; it also heals the communities that dwell in it. Only a few farmers keep horses and cows in sufficient quantities: the best muck-heaps therefore result from cooperation, and form durable knots in the web of rural barter. Our own is the work of three neighbouring farms, and has the character of an institution, con-

tributing to the difficult but ever necessary work of restoration –
replenishing not only the top-soil of Sundey Hill, but also the
social top-soil of our little community.

Nitrogen creates soil too rich and grass too tall for shy meadow flowers, and the over-use of muck will have the same effect.
Hence few of our fields are sprinkled as once they were with corn-
flower, poppy, eyebright, vetch and harebell. The names still chime
with us, but the flowers have vanished. Virtually the only spring-
time colour besides the green on green of rye-grass, is the yellow of
crowfoot. Cows and horses will eat around this acrid buttercup,
leaving it to colonize the field.

Nevertheless, the wildflowers of the British Isles have not yet
followed the wolf to extinction. Along railway tracks, forest paths
and the verges of country lanes they grow wherever the sun can
reach them, and the first urge of every country-lover is to tell them
apart and to know their names. Wildflowers offer a glimpse into
the vanished world of simples and charms. Their names are not
scientific labels but spells: invocations of occult powers. Some tell
us directly of their use: all-heal, goutweed, sneezewort, knitbone,
eyebright and wolfsbane, which helped to rid our country of the
wolf. Others are more allusive, suggesting spiritual as well as physical refreshment: woodruff, hyssop, saxifrage, arnica, yarrow, milk-
vetch, chamomile and meadowsweet. Our ancestors believed that
medicinal plants were shown to mankind by the angels – hence the
name 'angelica' for the one that helped them most.

Plants in general, and flowers in particular, formed the crucial
link between the animal and the mineral world. They were the soothing and enchanting potions that connected us again to Mother
Earth. Shakespeare, whose verse is full of spells, understood this.
The names of flowers occur repeatedly in his plays, sometimes
placed side by side with their spiritual meaning (as by Ophelia),
but sometimes left to stand alone, mysterious syllables in which we
hear an echo of the ancient dialogue between earth and man, so
that (as Kipling later expressed it):

Almost singing themselves they run:
Vervain, Dittany, Call-me-to-you –
Cowslip, Melilot, Rose of the sun ...

In Shakespeare's day the lore of plants was not only a powerful
stimulus to the imagination but also a living source of knowledge.

Medicine had few resources beyond the wisdom of previous generations – a wisdom acquired over centuries, through trial and suffering. That wisdom has since been vaporized by science, and few of
our country residents have retained any trace of it. One exception is
Lynn, who breeds shire horses and pedigree sheep on her little farm
in the valley past our church. Here wild flowers grow in abundance
on high banks beside the lane, and Lynn collects them and distils
them into essences. For colds she makes a brew of hyssop and for
headaches another of feverfew. And in these cordials are dissolved
not only the remedial juices of the flowers but also their soothing
names, which work on the spirit and coax it along healing paths.

Her greatest triumph to date, however, has been her cure for
equine arthritis. Horses and cows will turn up their noses at wildflowers and herbs, unless you dry them carefully, or ferment them
in darkness. Lynn's mixture for arthritis contains the dried leaves
of nettle, comfrey, dandelion and celery, and the dried roots of
burdock and elecampane. A few spoonfuls morn and night restored
old Barney, whose back legs had so stiffened that he could hardly
jump, to the full vigour of youth; he is still running with the field
and jumping in his twenty-first year.

Lynn's larder is like an old apothecary's shop, with jars of dried
woodruff and chervil, bottles of lavender oil, rosemary water, and
wood-sorrel gruel, jars of pastes and syrups and tinctures, and the
usual abundance of cordials, pickles and homemade wines. She is
the proof of John Ruskin's words, that 'no dying petal nor droop-
ing tendril is so feeble as to have no help for you'. She encounters
help in every hedgerow, and collects it for future use.

'There is brass in muck' is true enough as a piece of ready wisdom; but there is far more brass in clay, if you can get permission
to use it. Clay hollows are impermeable basins, into which you can
throw what you like, without fear that it will find its way into
neighbouring streams and rivers. They are therefore targeted by
waste-disposal firms. Since people produce ten times their own
weight in rubbish every year, rubbish dumps are now more valuable than building land. A farmer who can sell off his farm as a
land-fill site will become a millionaire; and five years later, when it
is all grassed over, he could return to his old house to live in style
– were it not for the angry neighbours.

One nearby resident has been trying for years to sell his farm
for such a use; whenever the planning application comes up the

neighbours call meetings, write to the press, draw up petitions, and lobby the Council, referring to lorries on narrow roads, squalor, noise, health hazards, smells, ugliness, tattered plastic in the tree-tops, and hordes of rats under ground. Each time the Council is persuaded, and the application refused. And each time we become more aware of the damage that our modern habits do. The whole economy is now centred on junk – not only the packaging of food and drink, but the so-called 'consumer durables', which endure long after they have been consumed. Cars, refrigerators, radios, TVs, household gadgets – all, within a few years of purchase, reveal what they truly are and will henceforth remain, namely rubbish.

The scare over landfill sites has made us conscious of our wasteful habits: three bags of rubbish each week, much of it packaging from things that ought never to have been packaged except in old newspapers. We have been hoping to emulate our neighbours, the Morris family, whose sole offering for the dustman consisted until recently of a half-filled paper feed-bag, tied firmly with bailing twine like an old-fashioned purse. This bag represents a lifestyle not so much frugal as self-renewing: Mrs Morris grows her own vegetables, keeps geese and chickens for the table, and drinks the unpasteurised product of her cows, so that none of her family's food arrives in packaging. Nothing is wasted, and the family lives, so to speak, on ecological tiptoe.

That is not the opinion, however, of the local environmental officer, who loves to vent his regulatory zeal on farmers, and who has nosed out the effluent from Ted Morris's cows. Clay is both the problem and the offered solution. Being impermeable, the subsoil will not absorb waste, which therefore flows off into the ditches when sprayed on the field.

The solution, the bureaucrat tells us, is to dig a great hole on the top of Sundey Hill which, because of the wonderful properties of clay, will hold the stuff until it has rotted into garden fertilizer, cough mixture or gravy browning. The cost of this, however, has to be borne entirely by Ted, and his feelings in the matter run so high that he, as economical of words as he is of rubbish, and regarding both commodities in the same general light, waxes lyrical nevertheless for a good 15 minutes on the subject of environmental experts. Once or twice he has visited Swindon and seen with his own eyes what is permitted in the way of tips and debris and stagnant pools of poison. 'And they experts come worrying I

on account of they cows!' The injustice of this is compounded by
its evident irrationality, and Ted's faith in human beings, never very
great as befits a man who lives with more peacable animals, has
been profoundly shaken. Since the visit of the environmental officer there have been two brown paper bags each week for the dustman – diligently tied with bailing twine, but a sign nonetheless that
Ted is determined to earn his new reputation as an eco-bandit.

The world-wide distribution of food packages a product that is
necessary, renewable, and natural in vast amounts of unassimilable
waste. The global food economy therefore means a global rubbish
dump. It is not in the cities that this rubbish dump is most clearly
visible. The sterile layers that you tear from your supermarket
chicken go straight into the dustbin, and are carted away you know
not where. Occasionally you see a plastic bag hurrying along the
pavement on a windy day. And maybe you notice a school-child
throwing his empty cola bottle into the gutter. But these things
make little impression in an urban context, where everything is
man-made, and where the assumption is that rubbish will eventually be 'disposed of'.

However, plastic does not rot down or turn to topsoil; no
plants can take root in it or animals feed from it, and to burn it is
to fill the air with poison. The destiny of plastic, therefore, is to
move from place to place, unwanted and incorruptible, a permanent sign of man's usurpation. Sooner or later it will become visible – on a beach, in a ditch, in a hedgerow or suspended on the
branch of a tree. And there it will linger from week to week, until
blown to its next destination. Hence the global rubbish dump,
which is concealed from the city dweller, is gradually surfacing on
seashores and riverbanks, in fields and hedgerows, and in the
ditches of country lanes.

In the hedge before my window, high up in the branches of an
ash-tree, some plastic wrapping lodged last spring. It is still there,
flapping in the wind like pennants on the rigging of a man-o'-war.
In the field beneath it is an enormous black sheet, buried years ago
by top-soil but surfacing from time to time when a horse kicks
away the earth or catches a corner in his teeth while grazing. In
the ditches along our road are plastic bottles, sweet wrappers and
cellophane sandwich boxes, carelessly thrown down by passing
motorists. A large plastic drum containing creosote appeared last
winter in Iris pond, floating from nowhere and tangling in the

rushes where the mallards nest. Other relics – oil cans, plastic gloves, syringes, bailing twine, strips of sheeting – lie beneath the hedgerows, and here and there the effect is amplified by slovenly farmers, who allow the black wrappings from their silage bales to drift across the road and festoon the dead branches of the elm trees. On windy days you see those lasting products of the global food economy, and symbols of its ubiquitous triumph – the platoons of polythene carrier-bags, embellished with the logo of some supermarket chain, and hurrying from treetop to treetop 'like ghosts from an enchanter fleeing'. Apparently some 150,000 tonnes of these bags are consumed in Britain each year – not consumed in fact, but released into the landscape, in search of their permanent home.

The permanent and uncorrodable is not in itself offensive, else we should never rejoice, as we do, in rocks and stones and barren hillsides. Nor is all manmade waste disturbing: rusting tools, discarded rags, cast-iron tanks and abandoned farm machinery all have their charm, and all become mellow with age and gradually blend with the landscape. What offends in plastic is the danger that we read in it. Here is something man-made but made to outlast us; something that is in its very essence waste; something inert, alien, on which life can neither feed nor take root, a spectral visitor that adds nothing to the order that it haunts, but which poisons all that it touches. The countryside today reminds you of William Empson's lines:

Slowly the poison the whole bloodstream fills.
The waste remains, the waste remains and kills.

Those who throw away their sandwich wraps or cola bottles do not merely offend the human eye; they offend all of nature – the plants stifled by the airless sheets that lie on them, the insects trapped by sugar-filled bottles, the foxes and badgers which, attracted by the meaty scent of a cellophane sandwich box, die horribly from a blocked intestine. In all these ways, the inertness of plastic, which causes it to stand apart from the natural world, makes it deadly to creatures who depend on an environment that lives and dies as they do.

We too depend on that environment, and plastic reminds us of the enormous self-deception that lies at the heart of the global economy. It is the permanent record of the damage that we are doing to an order that can be damaged only so much, and only for so long. And it appears in our ditches and hedgerows, blown in from nowhere, addressing us with its mute impassive stare and making our somewhere into nowhere too.

Of a piece with plastic is the thing by which it is spread – the motor car. There is scarcely a person in this country who has not lost a friend, relative or acquaintance to the motor car, and, until they are actually inside it, enjoying the unreal power that comes from complete surrender to mechanism, people look on the car as a fearsome engine of destruction. Yet the motor industry continues to enjoy every subsidy that state or society can concoct for it. A peculiar, fictional economy has arisen, which requires people, food and animals to be sped round the earth on redundant journeys. Many of us consume half our lives, three-quarters of our energy and 99 per cent of our emotions in travelling, without once using our legs. And the effect of this on social life, on physical well-being, on childhood adventure and adult joy is incalculable.

The narrow roads around Sundey Hill are hardly frequented by traffic, and we can go from place to place by horse or bicycle. Occasionally, however, the main road from Malmesbury to Cricklade is closed, and the traffic diverted through our valley. Overnight everything changes. Our lanes are pedestrian precincts, made less for driving than for walking, with a narrow strip of roadway bordered by soft verges, and hedges arching overhead. Suddenly they are besieged by vans and hauliers racing to deadlines; by consultants driving with a mobile phone to the ear; by bus drivers with their cargoes of children's faces, flattened like posters against the glass – unfamiliar people, locked in conflict with the bends and hedgerows that to us had been the contours of a garden. The roadways are smeared with the carcases of deer, squirrels, foxes and badgers, the verges are churned to a soup of sterile clay, while the ditches fill with Walkers immortal crisp packets, and Tesco's deathless sandwich wraps.

There are those who argue that the best way to ensure peace on our country lanes is to build more roads. By-passes, motorways and relief roads absorb the inter-urban traffic, and free the lanes for local traffic. That is the official doctrine, and it is a comforting one, since it implies that things will improve. However it is false. Motorways and by-passes are the cause, not the effect, of traffic. Moreover, by driving on them, people adjust their reflexes to speed, and continue at speed long after they have left the slip road.

Malmesbury is crowded with both people and cars: pedestrians and drivers share the street, each weaving past the other without fear of a collision. This peaceful coexistence of people with the thing that principally threatens them is an effect of narrow winding streets and awkward angles, of steep hills and blind corners. And the calming effect of Malmesbury would be felt in all the surounding villages, had it not been for the mad decision to build a by-pass to one side of the town. The lesson of this by-pass, which has destroyed so much life in our local villages, is that roads should not be widened but narrowed. One day, when driving has become futile, people will step from their cars and totter on trembling and unpractised legs towards their destination. And they will discover that their destination is not there, where they were going, but here, where they are.

Our narrow roads have another significance for us. In the normal run of things they are not conduits through which strangers pass on their way to nowhere, but lifelines to the wider economy. The most important vehicle that navigates their curves is the milk tanker, which must come each day, and which must be big enough to take the daily harvest. However narrow or muddy the lane, the articulated cylinder must push its way through, and any delay threatens our local livelihoods. Not that there is money now in milk; nevertheless, ours is a dairy country, and there is no changing that fact without also changing the soil, the drainage, the landscape and the people, for whom milking defines the times, the spaces and the rhythms of their day.

The driver of the tanker is as wedded to the landscape as the farmers whom he visits, and the cows whose product he conveys. Although he has a tight schedule, and a vehicle that nobody would care to argue with, he slows down for children, dogs and horses, and will never run over a pheasant or a hare. His is the one heavy vehicle that no animal need fear, and in a strange way its metallic colours and unnatural shape have begun to blend with the landscape, and to symbolize the benign economy of which it is a functional part.

On the first morning of snow last year we awoke to find the roadway carpeted, the edges invisible, and only the tracks of animals puncturing its smooth veneer. The economy of the farm is to some extent helped by snow. The animals are all indoors and, with the ground now harder, the remaining jobs of autumn can be done. We can get the tractor into the fields to trim the hedges. We can spread the muck without getting axle-deep in clay. We can walk across the frozen bog to pick up the sheep-wire. And with the snow come those eager and unfamiliar birds: fieldfares, redwings and waxwings, swirling in flocks through the denuded trees. The entropic world beyond our lanes is suddenly shut off from us. No rat-running commuters, no fly-tippers, no tourists or nosy parkers: just us alone with our animals. It is therefore a time of work; but also a time of recuperation, when the work comes wrapped in self-sufficiency.

We walked around the farm, enjoying the silence and the landscape, whose manmade sores were hidden under a pure white bandage. A set of paw prints circled the chicken run, before heading for the road. Each mark was led by two needle points: the hard curved claws of a fox. We followed the spoor along the verge, and the prints became cleaner and fresher as we went. Then we saw him, standing in the roadway, his mask turned towards us, his fine red brush a-glitter with snow. Badgers, rabbits, hares and stoats never really look at you: their eyes serve another function, which is to capture information and bury it deep in the blood. Foxes, by contrast, bestow long, intense and calculating looks – looks full of an impregnable solitude. In the words of Ted Hughes:

> *an eye,*
> *A widening, deepening greenness,*
> *Brilliantly, concentratedly,*
> *Coming about its own business …*

We stood a hundred yards apart, exchanging mutual challenges. Those still yellow-green eyes conveyed a threat: leave a carcass by my earth, or you will regret it. We remembered the bones of the Christmas turkey, and made a mental note to make a gift of them.

As we stood thus mutely communing, the tanker, its wheels muffled by snow, came almost inaudibly round the corner, the driver wide-eyed with anxiety as he applied the brakes. The fox glanced up at him, gave a nod of recognition, and then skipped off the road, padding quietly into the hedgerow and up the hill. The driver greeted us, put his tanker into gear and drove on, embossing the roadway with its first mark of tyres.

It was an ordinary episode, but strangely poignant. The cold which made us mutually dangerous, made us also mutually respectful. The tanker crept along the road as though it had a right to the landscape. And all around us was a snow-bound stillness, beneath which the earth attended to our silent dialogue and recorded its terms. Man, animal and machine entered together into a pre-lapsarian state of belonging, and for a moment we were at rest in our re-imagined world.

Our narrow lanes are fragile too, and every now and then become impassable even to the tanker. Not far from here lies Braydon Pond, set among woodlands, already the largest pond in Wiltshire in John Aubrey's day, and expanded further to a lake in Victorian times. A lane runs past the water, travelling from nowhere to nowhere, and carrying only a few vehicles each day. The lane crosses a causeway, beneath which the overflow cascades into a stream and thence to the River Avon. Standing on this causeway you can watch the birds that have made their home on the water. There are winter visitors – widgeon, shelduck and snipe – and the marauding seabirds from our depleted shores. It is our local beauty spot, a place where lonely people feed the ducks, where others take their dogs and their children, where elderly couples rediscover romance, where you can ride a horse without being driven into the ditch, where you can stand and dream and listen to the lonely cry of the heron above the sound of running water.

Some time ago, following a succession of dry summers, the causeway began to subside. The local Council decided to close the road, to drain the pond, and to make a few repairs. For a year or more the pond stood almost dry, the herons feasting on the carp that thrashed in the muddy puddles. The shells of fresh-water mussels littered the cracked perimeter, and the lake revealed its store of jam jars, jerry cans, car tyres and bicycles. Soon, however, the job was abandoned and the Council decided that motorists would now need instructions to cross the narrow causeway. Vast metal signs were put up at 50-yard intervals, the first in red, announcing that new arrangements are approaching, the next also in red, saying that a sign will soon be visible, the third, triangular and in luminous yellow, announcing the imminence of a fourth sign, declaring that the road, which is visibly wide enough for only one vehicle, is indeed wide enough for only one vehicle. At this point a final sign appears, exhorting the driver to give way to oncoming traffic – traffic that is certain not to exist, and which in any case has to descend a hill in complete visibility for half a mile before reaching the causeway. The same sequence of hysterical signs ascends the hill on the other side, the whole amounting to some thousands of pounds' worth of junk metal in loud primary colours, situated at the one sensitive point where the beauty of the pond can be appreciated, and so removing the only reason why anyone would want to come this way in the first place.

Road signs constitute both an arrogant invasion of privacy and a destruction of public space. Braydon Pond was a communal place, where people would pass each other with polite words and genial nods, recognizing their equal title to a shared tranquillity. Now it is overlooked by instructions, thrown out with the visual equivalent of a sergeant-major's bark, designed not to harmonize but to be dissonant, to abolish tranquillity, and to unsoothe and unsettle the soul. Braydon Pond, they tell us, is not yours but no-one's.

Above Braydon Pond there stands another such intrusion: a modernist water-tower in white concrete, whose pilotis-legs protrude jaggedly into the skyline, and whose unsupported drum looms above the treetops, cowering us with the thought of a second Flood. All who pass this object avert their eyes, and houses from which it can be seen sell for less than those that are spared the sight of it. It does not belong in the landscape, will never be regarded as a 'landmark', and cannot be, as hilltops otherwise are, the goal of a country ramble or the site of a picnic. Like the road signs on the hill below, it belongs to a growing habit of rudeness, being designed to stand out rather than to fit in. This rudeness can be observed in every use of public space, whether landscape or townscape. Shop signs and adverts no longer petition for a modest share of a space acknowledged to be everyone's, but loudly assert their self-centred monopoly over a space that they also declare to be no-one's.

Things were not always so. Notices used to be composed in sober lettering, shop fronts and street signs would be discreet, dignified and withdrawn, deferring to the public space and stopping at its threshold. If they had an imperative message, then they put on a uniform, like the coat of arms on the village post office. There was a general recognition that human society is a delicate thing, which must take precedence over any cry for attention. This deference towards the public realm was not destroyed by the industrial revolution. On the contrary, it shaped the forms of industrial architecture, just as it had shaped the church, the town hall and the country house.

Hence, even these isolated and necessary things, in which nobody dwells, were once built to resemble habitations, which were not dumped in the landscape but settled there. The tops of

Victorian water towers were moulded and crenellated; their sides were cased in masonry, and at the place where they touched the ground a fairy door would open onto stairs winding to the summit past windows that broke the expanse of wall. Better even than the water towers of the Victorians were those built by the Hapsburg officials in their drive to bring the amenities of modern life to the disgruntled people of the Empire. All over Central Europe you will find these pillars of centralized authority, sturdy symbols of order and settlement in the midst of change. One such tower, in the southern suburbs of Prague, became a centre of resistance during the last years of communism. For it was in this tower that the authorities had confined the dissident philosopher Daniel Kroupa as night-watchman, having forbidden him all other employment. The tower became part of the secret campus of the underground university, from which students took away memories not only of the learning and culture that had been officially forbidden, but also of a civilized architecture that breathed the same spirit as the books they read. For those whose alma mater it now is, the Horní Roztyly water tower is as much a symbol of European culture as the Oxford colleges. And this tower reminds us of a simple principle, which is that buildings look right in the countryside, if they would look right in a town. For the only thing that ever looks right in either place is the human decision to dwell there.[25]

Water towers illustrate an important architectural principle, which is that the sky is as much a part of the landscape as the earth, and that buildings can damage the sky even more than they damage the land. The caps, pinnacles, finials and crenellations that were once obligatory were wonderful habitats for birds, and one of the reasons why our towns were filled with birdsong. But they also had a social and spiritual function, which was to slot the building into the heavens, and thereby to attach it more firmly to the earth. This is part of what appeals to us in the pitched roof and decorated chimney; it is what leads us to demand mouldings, ornaments and human details in any building that stands higher than its neighbours. And it is what is most evidently missing from the jagged disorder of wires and discs and ariels that is now sprouting on every English hilltop.

The problem is illustrated in another way by petrol stations, which in our neighbourhood are the last remaining rural shops, simultaneously blots on the landscape and centres of rural life.

Petrol stations owe this dual identity to the fact that they are owned by global corporations but managed by local residents. The corporations are indifferent to local character; the managers are part of it. The petrol station therefore represents a coming together of the global and the local, in a form that has much to teach us about the future of both.

Two characteristics of the petrol station make it an unwelcome guest in the countryside: the intrusive signs, ruder by far than those at Braydon Pond, and the horizontal panoply, which mutilates the village skyline. The first principle in architecture is that buildings should stand – a principle illustrated by the classical orders, by Gothic churches, by Georgian country houses and Victorian terraces; even by Bovis Homes. The canopy of the petrol station does not stand. It is a thing in motion, temporarily hovering by the roadside. It is designed to negate the restful character of its surroundings, to rebuke them for their homeliness, and to redesign the countryside as a place for speeding through.

One simple amendment to the planning laws would rectify this aesthetic disaster, and that is to insist that the canopy should have a pitched roof. For the pitched roof restores the vertical emphasis, negates the streamlined horizontal, and brings the whole structure to a state of visual order and psychic rest. It turns a symbol of flight into a symbol of dwelling.

Failing that amendment, it is better to have no canopy at all. Such is the case with our local petrol station. This building consists of three pumps in the courtyard of an old stone farmhouse. Behind the house is a large wooden shed, where repairs are carried out, and next to it another shed, in signal-box colours and with moulded fenestration, where vegetables, sweets and bottled drinks are sold across a wooden counter.

This station is not owned by the petrol company, but by Des, the manager, whose ancestors lie buried across the road, beneath the medieval church that casts its shadow on the courtyard. Des cannot afford a canopy and besides, his traditional customers never wanted one. The newcomers sometimes suggest this improvement; but Des is fairly sure that they will soon be buying their petrol, as they buy everything else, in the supermarket. Meanwhile the garage goes on fulfilling its old rural function, supplying gossip, fuel and emergency rations to a community increasingly cut off from the world beyond the motorway.

Des's petrol station is one of those places between town and country where you encounter the creative nature of their interchange. If you really want to understand the relation between town and country, you should study the places where they meet – not only village petrol stations, but scrubby wastelands on the edges of things, horse-sick paddocks by the motorway, run-down farms that are really garages, the last bungalows on the new estates, where geese and ducks spill out into the fields.[26] One such place is our lay-by, where town people come to renew their dreams and discard their rubbish, and where country people come to scavenge what remains.

The lay-by is situated at the top of the hill, with a distant view of Malmesbury. Rolling fields and hedges form an apron before it, and a dense copse descends into the valley beyond. In spring bluebells, stitchwort and cowslips grow along the edges; giant oaktrees make a shield from the western wind, and a pile of road grit tells you in a friendly way that this is a useful space, part of the rural economy, visited by others and not only by you. In the middle, by the hedge, sharply outlined against the landscape, is a large crimson armchair in mock-leather, solitary relic of a three-piece suite. Its shape, colour and materials clash horribly with the soft greens of the hedgerow, and the velvet texture of the pastures.

This armchair arrived overnight without an explanation. It invites you to pause, to sit in this corner of holy Albion, to take stock of nature and its uses, and to dictate some useless platitude. It also has a story to tell, and the story of this armchair is the story of our fields.

For many visitors to our lay-by the countryside is a place to be seen: they park by the hedge, wind down the window, and stare. For others it is a place where not to be seen – at least not by the neighbours. They come in their separate cars, and then sneak together into the back of one of them.

Youths arrive from Swindon, to sit whey-faced and motionless in their crowded mini-cars, deadening their brains on cannabis and techno. Other regulars merely walk their dogs, eat their sandwiches, or take stock of the world. The postman and the milkman park here each morning; one reads the paper, drinks tea from a thermos, and smiles at the birds, the other counts his bottles. Once a week Bernard, who runs an illegal haulage business, unhitches a trailer and leaves it standing, its jack sinking into the sun-softened tarmac. His containers have obscure Dutch and Italian markings, and nobody asks him what they have inside. Once in a while a stolen car is dumped here and set alight.

You cannot live in the vicinity of this place without concluding that the relation between town and country is both fertile and precarious. Our lay-by is a kind of market. Grit, scalpings and pipes from the town are dropped off for local uses. Goods are bought and sold, with or without the law's approval. And that which the countryside offers in return – space, air, wildlife, landscape and solitude – is freely available. The lay-by joins us to the world of commerce, craft and crime, and in return has nothing to offer save peace.

One summer's day two years ago we came across an old gypsy waggon parked in the lay-by, with maroon panels, red wheels and a dark canvas top. A smaller waggon in the same carnadine colours stood beside it, together with an antique trailer piled with pans and tools. Three shaggy ponies were tethered to the verge, and multi-ethnic chickens scratched and pecked along the hedgerow. A woodfire smouldered between the shafts of the larger waggon, with an old black kettle emitting cheerful gouts of steam. Smoke curled from a chimney in the waggon's roof, and the sunlight, trapped in the polished paintwork, set the whole scene ablaze. No detail of this scene was more charming for us than the large painted sign on the wagon's side, saying 'Work Wanted'. For that day Terry, our jack of all trades, had declared himself definitively sick and in need of a few days rest.

We came to negotiate. Inside the larger waggon, warming themselves by a cast-iron burner, were John and his pregnant wife, Mazzie. Not in the first flush of youth, but maybe still in the second, John spoke with a cockney accent, wore a bunch of silver earrings in his left ear, and dressed in the loose black clothes and armoured boots of a street urchin. He had been travelling for two years, he told us, and was making his way slowly to Wales, where he knew a wheelwright who could repair his wonky axles. Unfortunately, the wheelwright seemed to be a post-modern practitioner of this pre-modern craft, and was currently hang-gliding somewhere on the Costa del Sol. With time on their hands, John and Mazzie had decided to look round for some cash. They didn't need cash as others needed it, John added; but all the same they needed it.

For the five days that it took Terry to recover, John worked for us, carrying, forking, heaving, mending and managing in his own untroubled way. He was typical of his kind: not a gypsy or a migrant, but a version of Hardy's reddleman, moving from place to place in search of work, managing the hardships of road-life and enjoying the companionship of his wife and dog and ponies. He had done many jobs, but none of a settled kind, since settling was no part of his plans. Animals were instantly at ease with him and he with them; farmers welcomed him and offered water and hay. All along the road he collected things that others considered worn out or redundant, but which he could use or sell. His speech was gentle, his manner firm, his attitude to life that of an observer rather than a participant.

The most striking thing about John, however, is that nobody objected to his presence, despite the hostility towards travellers that is endemic to farming communities. This was not merely because John was a law-abiding person; nor was it only because he could offer labour on the unencumbered terms that the State forbids. It was because John's presence did not violate the landscape. His little train of wagons embellished the place where it stood, and acknowledged it as other people's territory. People smiled instinctively on seeing it, and waved a greeting as they passed.

There is an important truth to be gleaned from this. Every now and then in our stretch of country someone parks a mobile home by the roadside. And whenever this happens the locals write angry letters to the council, urging it to apply the law. The reason is simple. Modern mobile homes desecrate the places where they stand. This is a matter not just of colours and materials, but also of meaning. The mobile home has a provisional character; it is indifferent to its surroundings and designed to speed through them. If it should stay put nevertheless, it is with an air of stagnant impermanence, like the desultory towers of the post-war housing estate. Parked in open country the mobile home unsettles the landscape, cancelling its deep-down meaning as a home. At the same time it lays claim to the very territory to which it refuses to belong, endowing it with its own provisional and discarded character. In the vicinity of the mobile home even the landscape is junk.

Although John is not settled, he is not unsettled either. His wag-gons speak of slow, rhythmical movement. They are shaped to the earth and to the pace of earth-bound creatures. When they pause they seem to borrow the contours of the countryside, making it more not less of a home to its permanent residents. The waggons circulate through the lanes as though part of the great breathing organism which lies all around them, taking the oxygen of labour from farm to farm. Their dark red colour is reminiscent of blood, and their function too is blood-like, refreshing the landscape and swelling its veins.

John and Mazzie learned their way of life from gypsy lore. And by their unassuming and peacable manner they draw attention to the malevolent way in which the gypsy image is now exploited. Nearby Minety has recently been invaded by an organized gang of self-styled 'gypsies' who, having purchased a field from a farmer, arrived one night with bulldozers, pick-up trucks and caravans to install themselves as permanent occupants. The topsoil was scraped away and sold, the field was covered in concrete, and a score of white and cream caravans now destroy the view for which other and more law-abiding incomers paid all that they had and for the sake of which they have been prepared to accept the strict planning controls that limit what they can do with their property. As for the 'gypsies', they neither obtained planning permission nor sought it. The attempts by the local Council to enforce the order for agricultural use are now stalled by a legal claim that, under human rights legislation, gypsies have a 'right' to their vagrant lifestyle, and therefore a right to bypass laws designed to control the habits of more fortunate people. This kind of racist argument is being increasingly used, even though our law is supposed not to distinguish the rights and duties of different races, and even though few of those who are squatting in Minety can lay claim to an ancestry that is in any way more gypsy than mine.

This novel eruption of global entropy into our local order reminds us of the way in which the true gypsies of England have been assimilated. After cruel oppression under Queen Elizabeth I, they became shy nomads, living for the most part on the wrong side of the law, but never drawing attention to themselves so far as to awaken the kind of collective hostility which their putative cousins experience in Central Europe. By the time, a century and a half ago, when George Borrow went to live with them and record their ways, 'gypsyism' as he called it was in decline, the Romany language was fading, and the children of gypsies were looking for settled trades.

Almost nothing remains of the gypsy culture recorded and romanticized by Borrow. The pagan religion, the eclectic language (with one word meaning both life and death, and another both yesterday and tomorrow), the raggle-taggle costumes, and the vagrant ways – all have been traded for less dissonant habits. Those who maintain the real gypsy customs are as much urban incomers to the vagrant life as we are urban incomers to the life of the farmer. Their gypsy veneer is an urban phenomenon – which is not to say that it is phony or even skin deep. But it is a product of Borrow, fairgrounds and cod anthropology; people like John and Mazzie are as English as I am (though, like Sylvia Plath, I may be a bit of a Jew); monogamous and law-abiding. In fact they conform to the surrounding culture in all particulars, save only the need to wander. And when they wander, they do so discreetly, not staying for long in one place, and conscious that their quaint old waggon is part of the scenery. Study these innocent people, and you will realize that the attempt to 'racialize' our gypsies is based on a self-serving fiction, an invention of global politics that has nothing to do with the settled order of the English countryside, into which our real gypsies melted long ago, and into which our new age travellers are melting in their turn.

This settled order is what our planning laws were designed to perpetuate. In 1937 a group of our leading intellectuals – including E.M. Forster, J.M. Keynes and H.J. Massingham, under the leadership of the architect Clough Williams-Ellis, builder of Portmeirion – published *Britain and the Beast,* warning against the ribbon development that was not only eating up the countryside, but also making people entirely dependent upon the motorcar. After the war, very late in the day, action was taken, and the Town and Country Planning Acts imposed Green Belts around the towns and severely restricted all new building in the countryside.

Fifty years later we see that the effect of those planning laws has been to push up the price of country properties to the point where the old rural population cannot afford to stay on the land, and to ensure that whatever new building occurs in the country-side, it will be for the benefit of urban commuters, whose dependence on the motor-car will therefore be greater than ever. Moreover, there has been no stop to ribbon development. Instead of houses, which at least have the merit that their owners care for them and police their precincts, we have a growing trail of 'pony paddocks', which are not only more unsightly, with their barbed wire, shacks and half-cared for animals, but also a far greater inroad into the rural ecology.

Why is it that so many people respond with dread to new building in the countryside? What exactly do they fear? Some ascribe this fear to 'nimbyism' – a selfish desire to hold on to privileges that ought in justice to be shared. Recent planning issues in our village convince me that this is rarely so. Sidney, for example, has joined a campaign – so far unsuccessful – to persuade the Council to allow a field next to his farm to be given over to a 'self-build' scheme, so as to provide affordable housing for the young people who, against all the odds, are still produced in our village. Only half a century ago our farm had four cottages, all of which could be rebuilt without loss of amenity if permission were forthcoming. People know that it is irrational to go on farming when farming doesn't pay. Hence they accept the need to diversify. Most are quite happy to see light industry and warehousing in the countryside, provided it does not spoil what they love. One of the most picturesque areas of our neighbourhood is the Stroud Valley, with its line of stone-built mills and industrial hamlets mediating between the sheep-farms above and the wooded river below.

If we regarded the countryside as we do the wallpaper in a hotel bedroom, we should flinch at ugliness but learn to live with it. But the countryside means more to us than that. It is an icon of our homeland, a symbol of belonging, and a reminder of our civic ties. It is history naturalized and nature made historical. It touches us in all the obscure places where mystery, piety and the sacred still have a home. And what we fear is desecration.

Of course, being shy, sceptical and intimidated by sneers, we do not use words like 'sacred' and 'desecration'. We speak instead of 'eyesores'. Nevertheless, when we refer to an eyesore we really mean a soulsore. If people are distressed by pylons, by wind farms, and by the windowless, metal-clad buildings that grow along the motorways like spores it is because these things violate the landscape and cancel its meaning as a home. Hence they are perceived as litter.

In this they are quite unlike the early industrial architecture, and in particular unlike the Victorian railways, which embellished our country with viaducts, stations and railway hotels that are every bit as gentle in their aspect and public-spirited in their intention as the architecture of Georgian Bath. Kemble, our local station, is an impressive example. Two single-storey buildings of Cotswold stone, with Tudor arches and pattern-book mouldings, are linked by a cast-iron bridge across the railway. Each platform is sheltered by a roof, raised on perforated spandrels above gaily painted gothic columns. On one side is the former stationmaster's house; on the other the ticket office and waiting room, where a round Victorian table of pinewood bears copies of *Country Life*. An arch leads from the London platform into a little garden, and in the days when the trains and the station still belonged to the stationmaster, he planted this garden with shrubs and flowers for no other reason than that he liked them and believed that the passengers would like them too.

Next to the station stands the railway inn, still owned and managed by Arkell's, our local brewery, and in front of the inn a row of Wellingtonias sighs in the wind in winter and bubbles with birdsong in spring. Waiting on the platform at Kemble you can still enjoy the sounds and sights of travel as they were recorded by Edward Thomas and Thomas Hardy, in the days of the Great Western Railway. And you are reminded of the fundamental truth about travel: that it is a mistake. Don't leave, but stay – that is the message of Kemble – and make where you stay a home. This place was the stationmaster's castle, which was also open to all who lived here: not a point of departure but a point of return.

Kemble station illustrates a principle which, if uniformly adhered to, would reconcile people to the decline of farming and to the new uses of the countryside: the principle that it doesn't matter what you build, or for what purpose, or where, so long as it fits. Fittingness – what Alberti, in his great treatise on architecture, called *concinnitas* – is not a matter of visual appropriateness only. It involves a harmony between buildings and people, and between both and the landscape. It involves adapting a place to our uses and our uses to the place. In short, it is the public aspect of settling, and the visible commitment to a local way of life.

At a certain point in Stendhal's *Le Rouge et le Noir* the hero, Julien Sorel, makes a journey to England. He is appalled by the barbarous manners, the lack of sophistication and the gross diet of the natives, and at the same time astonished by the one redeeming feature of their country, which is the indescribable sweetness of the landscape. And he seems to recognize what we all now know, that this sweetness is not the natural product of the soil but the laborious and delicate by-product of centuries of peaceful settlement, in which fields and towns were hardly ever laid waste by warfare, in which independent farmers and settled landowners cared for their domains as trustees, and in which the rule of primogeniture ensured that farms, estates and villages passed on intact.

The most vivid symbol of this proces is the hedgerow – which lays a living web of ownership across the land. In Slavonic languages a hedge is a *zhivy plot* – a 'living fence', though following communist collectivization few of them are left in the places where Slavonic languages are spoken. Not only are hedges alive; they also *contain* life – more life, perhaps, than the woods and coverts that they join. They fill our crowded countryside with animals and birds, providing food, shelter and protection. Hedges are, perhaps, the most significant concession that man has made to other species, in his relentless search for territory. The hedge is also a symbol of community, a testimony to long-standing agreements over boundaries.

To be stockproof a hedge must be properly maintained. Where you see hedges that have grown straggly, with the trees wrestling upwards for the light, you know that the land is passing from the old grassland agriculture, in which sheep and cows were the main source of livelihood, to the new, in which horses, kept for the pleasure of urban refugees, have colonized the pasture. Horses are herd animals, but they do not move in a crush; each insists on his space, and defends it against encroachment. Hence horses can be confined with the flimsiest of wooden fences, while cows and sheep, which move in seething multitudes, will break down any barrier that is not able to withstand the combined weight of the herd. Where hedgerows are maintained, therefore, it is because of the business of meat and milk, which surrounds us here in the Wiltshire claylands. A properly matted hedge, armoured with thorns, and rooted over centuries, will withstand any number of panicking cows. Moreover, while a 'dead' fence is always getting weaker, a 'living' fence strengthens from year to year.

But when hedges have been allowed to riot upwards, they must be cut back and laid. Hedge-laying is a winter job, to be completed before the sap begins to rise. You need thorn-proof boots and trousers, a bill-hook for trimming, and a saw. You cut through the base of the larger growths to within an inch of the bark, before pulling them down and binding them together, as near to horizontal as you can. But you must know which growths to cut away entirely; which will be strong enough to form the central structure, which will encourage the hedge to grow inwards into its own mysterious darkness, instead of outwards to the light. Elms especially are a problem; do you bind them into the hedge, even if they are soon to die? Or is it true, as some suggest, that Dutch elm disease strikes only when the tree has risen 20 feet above its roots, which it can never do when bound in a hedge? The old lore of hedge-laying – and there is plenty of it – is silent on this crucial point. But we have no choice; without the elms, our hedges would not exist, so we must lay them.

A rule of thumb, known after its inventor as Hooper's Rule, tells us that we should count one century for every species that a hedge contains (ignoring the brambles and climbers that come in from outside).[27] Laying the hedge on Hanging Hill we have dis-covered blackthorn, elm, ash, hawthorn, elder, crab apple, hazel and privet. All our hedges deliver a similar count, from which we assume that they were planted, not after the Enclosure Act, but in the early Middle Ages, when all this land belonged to the Abbot of Malmesbury.

And this shows us what boundaries have meant to the English. They are not there to assert absolute rights of ownership against the stranger, but to divide the land for husbandry. Impermeable to beasts, they are permeable to people, who enjoy footpaths and rights of way that link farm to farm across the hedgerows. The true rural boundary is not an absolute 'no' like the padlocked gate on the pony paddock; it is a qualified 'yes', the sign of a shared way of life and a common history.

Our landscape abounds in trees, which occur along the hedgerows, grouped together in copses and often standing alone and minatory in the middle of the fields. Oak and ash are self-seeding, the spontaneous product of the hedgerows, indifferent survivors of our hopes and fears. But scattered across the country-side are those pools of colour where the species riot – silvery horn-beam, golden chestnut and yellow poplar, red and purple maple, and occasionally the vibrant fruit of firethorn and cotoneaster. Wherever these copses blaze, you know that a human being has staked a claim to be remembered. These are the gardens of van-ished farms and cottages or the plantations and parklands which once radiated from a country house; they owe their being to an act of faith, and have survived not only the death of the people who planted them, but also the ruin of their houses and the destruction of a way of life which those people imagined would go on forever.

There are two reasons for planting a tree: to remember, or to be remembered. When people die before their time, we try to soothe our troubled feelings by investing in the future, and what better investment than a tree that will stand firm against the elements for centuries, but which is nevertheless a living, breathing, spirit-haunted thing? Such acts of remembrance have made their mark on the landscape; but a far greater mark has come from the plea to be remembered, which arises when people become aware of their mortality, and begin planting and possessing a plot of their own. In the field next door – Dollakers – there once stood a cottage, built perhaps by Doll herself. All that we know of this, apart from a few half-buried flagstones, is the little copse of mixed shrubs and berries, amid which stood a pear. Every year after my arrival here this great tree would flower in the spring, dropping its small unripened fruit in summer. Its tresses flowed in the autumn wind, and the leaves would be scattered over the backs of the sheep which in autumn nibbled what was left of the pasture. This tree was all that memory retained of Doll and when, in last year's winter storms, it crashed to the ground, Doll's spirit finally relinquished its territory. For the first time we felt free to plant the garden that had been hers.

More presumptious than Doll's pear tree are the monuments built to themselves by wealthy people. Robert Holford, having made a fortune in the water industry, decided 130 years ago to imprint his mark on the landscape in the time-honoured English way. The result was the country seat of Westonbirt, which was to perpetuate the spirit of Holford for centuries to come. The great house is now a school; its dependent cottages are inhabited by telecommuters; and the famous Westonbirt arboretum is owned by the Forestry Commission and maintained as a public park. Had Holford envisaged this result, he might never have begun the arduous work of collecting and transplanting species. But he lived at a time when hereditary property was a right – indeed, a duty, a way of rescuing wealth from decay. He could project his plans beyond the grave, precisely because his memory was enshrined in his property, and his property could be left to his heirs. Death duties, gift taxes, and taxes on wealth have ensured that almost nothing of significance now passes from generation to generation. Things can endure in the modern world only if they are owned by things that endure. And it is *things*, not people, that endure. Hence much of the countryside is owned by impersonal bodies like the Forestry Commission and the National Trust.

Those permanent bureaucracies are not dwellers in the landscape but absentee landlords. Although Westonbirt is well maintained by the Forestry Commission, the Commission itself would never have planted such a useless thing as an arboretum. Only private individuals, faced by their mortality, can encompass these death-defying gestures. The Commission, founded to provide timber in times of national emergency, produces a monoculture of Christmas trees; it has no interest whatsoever in leaving a monument to posterity. Likewise the National Trust, despite being devoted to monuments, is in the business of embalming them. It too could never create the things that it conserves, and, by soothing our anxieties over the future of the countryside, the Trust makes acceptable the taxes that are wiping it away.

Our part of the world has fared better than most. We still have our great park and our Jacobean mansion. We still have our soothing estate, with its walls and avenues and dependencies, with its outlying farms and woodlands and its cottages clustered in the fields. I say 'we' and 'our' deliberately: for, being in private hands, these things belong more fully to the landscape and to the people who live there than any property run by the Great and the Good from their offices in London. Charlton Park is a living part of the local economy, a source of pride and work and profit, which inoffensively maintains the old image of England without a trace of Ye Olde Aspicke purveyed by the National Trust.

The recent history of Charlton Park is a useful reminder that adaptation, not freezing, is the best way to conserve what we value. When the umpteenth Earl of Suffolk and Berkshire, having distinguished himself in the service of his country with acts of dare-devil heroism, was finally killed while attempting to dispose of a German bomb, his son was six years old. Although the dead Earl was killed in action, and although a whole section of the Park was requisitioned as a camp for prisoners of war, it was still decreed that the full measure of death duties must be exacted from the trustees. The farms were already out to rent, and the house was occupied by a girls' school, which went bankrupt after the war (with an unpaid quarterly bill at the local wine merchant for 17 gallons of gin). By the time the new Earl could inherit the 5,000 acre estate – all that remained of the vast expanse acquired by the Earl's ancestor

William Stumpe when he purchased the Abbey lands at the Dissolution – it was entirely encumbered by profitless leases, with a residual capital of £2,000. Lord Suffolk was advised to hand the whole lot to the National Trust, who were offering £28,000 as a full and final settlement. He decided instead to make a go of it.

Bit by bit the present Earl repossessed his territory, turning the farms to profit, selling off cottages (Sunday Hill Farm included), converting the Jacobean mansion into flats. Charlton awoke from its coma, to become the collective home of new and appreciative residents, with a populous village tied by social and economic interest to the Park. The great courtyard was rented to Polly Williamson, the champion eventer, who installed her horses in the stables and her grooms in the lofts above. The malthouse became a nursery school, or 'ghoul' as Sam Scruton (an eager pupil) used to call it. The outlying ruined barns were restored and have now been turned into offices. If all 'business parks' had the appearance and the surroundings of the offices at Charlton Park it is certain that no-one would object to them. In 100 novel and not so novel ways Charlton Park has become what it was during 300 years of stewardship – the centre of the local economy. Through the Park the life of the soil is subsidized from the wider economy, without the intervention of the state.

Hence while the National Trust devotes itself to varnishing its mummies, Charlton continues to live. And you sense this in the ineffable peace that enfolds you as you enter the Park on a winter's day, when the last leaves lie scattered on the turf, when the rank of depleted maple trees stands above them like a battalion of guardsmen, when the mansion, the farmhouse, the stables and the outbuildings, standing firm and undamaged behind their protective apron, shed light from all their doors and windows, and when framed in them the busy forms of farmers, teachers, children, grooms, secretaries, welders, machinists and labourers cast dancing shadows on the grass.

It is to such premodern settings that postmodern people tend to gravitate. One such was Muriel (alias Roberta) Latow, a 300 pound predator from Manhattan, author of *Hungry Heart* and other novels, whose style is typified by the following:

> *He reached for the silver jug of thick cream that he had fetched from the dining table when he had left her for those few minutes. Still lost somewhere in the aftermath of orgasm*

she had hardly recovered as she watched the cream dribble slowly from the jug in a thin trail around the nimbus of her breasts. (For some reason breasts always have a nimbus.) *He dipped the jug and trickled a lazy stream of cream between her breasts, the flat of her belly, trailed it over her...*

Muriel had persuaded Lord Suffolk to lease her an old farm for life, in return for taking charge of its renovation. One glance at her physical condition was sufficient to persuade Lord Suffolk that this was an attractive offer. Muriel set about converting the farm into the set for a Woody Allen film, in which every space opened into every other and every vista terminated in a bed. Luring the premodern neighbours into her centrally-heated acreage she would impart to them her views on the finer uses of butter, cream and chocolate, while they anxiously searched for the vista that ended in a door. Shunting her great face like the bowsprit of a laden vessel across the parquet, the folds of ample flesh rustling and flapping beneath the sails of a silken garment, she would pour out oleagenous words that were as unrelated to the view from her window as the erotic paintings on the walls, or the piles of perfumed furs in every corner, before sinking onto the reinforced couch that occupied the centre of her enormous living space. Exhausted, she would stare in silence at her departing guest from beneath half-closed eyelids, nodding sadly in response to his hurried goodbyes.

Muriel died shortly after completing the restoration of the farmhouse, and Lord Suffolk was able to realize his, or rather her, investment. This, surely, is the way for our place to renew itself without losing its history, or its deep-down rural character – to use global madness to subsidize local sanity. Muriel's postmodern life conjured an immense amount of money from the airwaves, and brought it to earth exactly here, where it can maintain the lives of premodern people. It was not long before I decided to follow her example.

6

Our Future

Sometimes we take a few days' holiday in Moravia, not far from Veseli, the tiny hamlet in the forest where the tales of the Cunning Little Vixen were told. Our village once had a German majority. Fleeing from vengeful persecution in 1945, they had left their tidy farmsteads to the Czech-speaking peasants. Even today many of the old farmhouses stand empty, awaiting the nouveaux riches who will convert them into second homes.

Second homes they never were. Each farmstead is a first and only home, a self-sufficient castle, dedicated to its plot of land, to the family within its walls, and usually to the Holy Trinity, portrayed in bas-relief above the wooden doors that shut in the animals and shut out the thief. Behind these doors the farm is laid out in a horseshoe, with hayloft, cow-stall, pig-sty, stable, kitchen and living room all opening onto the central courtyard, where the winter dung-heap warms both man and beast. There is a room for geese, another for chickens, a third for the vehicles and tools of the farm. The kitchen is built around the bread oven, on top of which is a space for two people to sleep. In one corner is a stone vat, in which the plums were simmered into jam; in another is the copper still for making slivovitz. Cool cellars have been dug into the rocky subsoil, and apples, wine, fat, pickles and sausage would be stored here through the winter.

Such, at any rate, is the house that we borrow, and we pad around its precincts with a subdued awe, encountering nothing except objects explained by their old utility, which wear their vanished functions like haloes in this eerie afterlife. On the hill outside the house an old peasant – Mrs Němcová, whose name means German – comes each day to cut and turn the hay. The old habits of subsistence have survived here, held tight against the communist system as a coat is held against the wind. The communists hated no-one so much as the small farmer, who is proof of tradition against utopia, of piety against plans, and of the individual's ability to survive outside the state. That is why Stalin murdered 10 million of them, and why the Party took away from the peasant everything save the old tools that the communists judged to be useless, but which in fact enabled people to scrape a better living from their tiny patches than the conscripts of the *kolkhoz* could extract from hectare upon hectare of barren fields.

Mrs Němcová cuts with a scythe, and as she rises over the hillside, her broad Slavic face wrapped in a kerchief, her leggings tied with string beneath a cotton skirt, the soft melancholy sound of her reaping is like the quiet tread of death behind her. She is 81 now, has seen the worst that man can do, has lost a husband and a son, but still retains the gentle smile and nonsensical patter of the babička, as she pauses to cluck at baby Lucy, using all the sweet diminutives that her language affords.

I wonder whether I should help; but there is something in her stooped form that rebuffs quixotic chivalry. In any case, she soon puts down the scythe of her own accord, and comes to sit at the garden table. Her story does not need much coaxing. She lives now as she has lived since the end of the war, when a cottage and half an acre of orchard were allotted to her. She and her husband had no employment to gain from the communists, and no land to lose to them. During the communist years the collective farms brought collective failure. But here in the village the peasants lived as they had always lived, and wanted for nothing. Then as now Mrs Němcová bartered eggs for hay, and rabbits for beer. She slaughtered a pig in December, calling in the neighbours for the salting and smoking that would see them through the winter. The early autumn was devoted to jam, pickles, slivovitz and the bottling of fruit. She kept geese, ducks and hens to supply her wants by barter. The scythe, the rake and the wheelbarrow were the inoffensive props of her routine, and then as now she enjoyed the tacit complicity of her neighbours in sustaining an economy outside state control and immune to innovation.

Mrs Němcová resumes her scything, leaving me to ponder our life back home. Almost everything that she described would be illegal in England. I listen to the gentle swishing of the scythe in the flower-strewn meadow, and envisage the EU directives that must surely forbid such a dangerous implement, and which in any case would prevent an old woman from using it. And her crooked form seems suddenly full of defiance: it is not death that wields her scythe, but life – the life of a free being, whose body has been bent by the years, but whose spirit will not be bowed.

The effect of regulation is to drive the economy underground, where it takes on another and more ancient form. This happened in the communist world; it is happening now under the new form of global capitalism. Throughout the once law-abiding regions of northern Europe people have ceased to regard the shadow economy as criminal. According to recent research, more than half of Germans dabble in it, most small home improvements are carried out through it, and moonlighting now represents 15 per cent of the official GDP in both Germany and Britain – a figure that grows from year to year, in direct proportion to the burden of regulations and taxes.[28] This burden falls most heavily on the small businesses, small producers, small farmers and small shopkeepers. Hence the part of the economy that is most important to the life of the community is being forced underground.

The criminalization of the old moral economy took a radical step forward when a decree from Brussels – a decree that was not even debated in our Parliament – abolished our old weights and measures. Our neighbours received this as a profound shock. Hitherto they had measured wheat and barley in bushels, rather than metric tonnes, exploiting the fluidity of grain, so as to deal it out with a scoop, a bushel being eight gallons, or 64 pints. Moreover a bushel is the most that a man can easily carry, and the right quantity to fill a sack. It is as reasonable to measure wheat in bushels as it is to measure beer in pints, petrol in gallons, meat in pounds, fields in acres, and distances in miles. These measures derive from human nature, and from our continual encounters with the objects themselves. They are not arbitrary or irrational, since they reflect a long acquaintance with the earth and things produced by it. Far more arbitrary is the metric system, which derives from the biological oddity that people have 10 fingers.

The imperial system also records a feature of English commercial life that has been of the first importance in our history: namely, that we measure things not by adding, but by multiplying and dividing. The important numbers in the imperial system are those like 16 (divisible by 2, 4 and 8), and 12 (divisible by 2, 3, 4 and 6). Our old currency, like our old weights, was adapted to the habit of distributing, and not just accumulating, goods. And for the same reason it lent itself to barter and exchange.

When the French Revolutionaries imposed the metric system it was with the express purpose of stamping out the old customs of rural France, and abolishing the consensual economics whereby ordinary people survive without the help of bureaucrats. The spirit that came to power in France in 1789 is now at large in Brussels, and the effect is the same: a preference for the 'rational' over the reasonable, and for the central plan over the local custom. We are now seeing the result: a sudden loss of practical knowledge, as people struggle to re-discover by thinking what they knew by second nature, so finding themselves mired in endless and avoidable mistakes.

One such mistake has had dire consequences for our rural economy. An EU directive allows animals to be slaughtered only in the presence of a qualified vet. Interpreted loosely in Spain (so that words like 'qualified' and 'vet' are as precise as 'mañana'), this rule is interpreted exactly in Britain, with the result that all our small abattoirs have had to close, being unable to pay so highly qualified and so totally redundant a person. Abattoirs are now few and far between and, in consequence, when Foot and Mouth disease broke out in Northumberland, it was carried all over the country in a matter of days. In our neighbourhood the cost was bearable – six months of quarantine, and the slaughter of 100 pregnant ewes. For others it was the end of their farming.

When a farmer's entire stock is wiped out prematurely, money cannot compensate. The primary loss is not financial but emotional: more – it is an *existential* loss, a sudden translation of the farmer to another mode of being. Once the centre of his territory, with dominion over a hundred living creatures, he is now reduced to a bewildered stranger in a world that he does not know and where he has no guidance. His silent farmyard and empty stalls are a kind of dreamscape, where nothing answers to his voice or touch, and through which he wanders with the strange padded powerlessness of dreams. Where death was once part of an ever-flowing cycle of regeneration, it is now a final extinction of life and hope. The farm falls out of history and time, to become a memory.

The greatest loss that results from such man-made catastrophes is therefore not the short-term economic loss but the long-term loss of social capital. The settled community may not enjoy all the wealth and excitement that are delivered by the global economy; but the global economy is a short-term parasitic outgrowth of these long-term and committed forms of human industry. It is through settling that the most important fund of social capital is accumulated, and an unsettled world will be one in which inherited wisdom will be irretrievably dispersed.

Advocates of the global economy argue that it is an inevitable development of the capitalist system, and that it will spread freedom, prosperity and democracy around the globe. Much intellectual effort is wasted on such half-baked predictions, which are usually not predictions at all, but intentions in the minds of maniacs. By pretending to predict when you are really deciding, you exonerate yourself from blame. You describe your purpose as 'inevitable', 'irreversible', a part of 'progress'. Anyone who resists is 'anachronistic', 'reactionary', a victim of 'nostalgia'. It was in such unsettling language that the revolutions of the twentieth century were sold to their gullible consumers, and the 1000-year Reich and the socialist millennium notwithstanding, people go on mouthing this trash and go on believing it.

It is of course undeniable that nostalgia has perverted much that has been written about the countryside. Books like Flora Thompson's *Lark Rise to Candleford* and Laurie Lee's *Cider with Rosie*, which unfold a vellum map with gentle and regretful fingers, have had a disproportionate influence on our national consciousness. But there is a great difference between nostalgia, which invents a past in order to take refuge in it, and the historical sense, which treasures the past as a fund of social knowledge. The greatest epochs of human endeavour have been periods of inheritance, in which people have tried not just to live for the future but also to live up to the past.

In a celebrated book published just before the First World War, George Bourne, writing as George Sturt, lamented the loss of the old 'organic' community of rural England, which he at the same time proposed as a moral ideal that we must strive in some way to recapture.[29] Bourne's lament was subsequently taken up by other writers, and notably by the great literary critic F. R. Leavis, who singled out *Change in the Village* as a kind of touchstone, against which to measure the extent of modern cultural decline. Responding to Leavis's regretful pleas for the old common culture – which had produced the people described by Hardy, the songs and dances collected by Cecil Sharp, and the folkways mourned by H. J. Massingham – Raymond Williams made the following trenchant observation:

> If there is one thing certain about 'the organic community' it is that it has always gone. Its period, in the contemporary myth, is the rural eighteenth century; but for Goldsmith, in *The Deserted Village* (1770) it had gone; for Crabbe, in *The Village* (1783) it was hardly 'right and inevitable'; for Cobbett, in 1820, it had gone since his boyhood...[30]

I seldom agree with Williams, and usually agree with Leavis. About this all-important matter, however, it seems to me that Williams was right. Lamentation over the fate of the countryside is an enduring literary theme. It has its roots in species-feelings that are expressed equally in the myth of Eden, in vegetation cults, and in the love of animals. Williams could have gone further back than he did – to Piers Plowman, to Virgil's Georgics, perhaps even to Hesiod, by way of illustrating the fact that man's relation to rural life is one that has been tinged since the birth of cities with a poignant and ill-defined regret.[31]

This does not mean that things haven't changed in modern times, or that everything that happens in the countryside should be accepted without complaint. However, we should recognize that the farming 'crisis' is no novel event, but a recurring drama: none the less real for being repeated, nevertheless an event that farmers have a proven capacity to survive.[32] Moreover we should reject the metaphor of the 'organic' community as intrinsically misleading. Settlement is not a bond between the cells of an organism but an association of free beings, who treat each other as sovereign. It is the relation on which markets ultimately depend, and it thrives in rural areas because people are compelled to assume responsibilty for their own lives, in an economy that places a premium on trust.

However, Groucho's famous paradox – why should I want to belong to a club that would have *me* as a member? – applies in another form to settling. How can I settle among settled people without unsettling them? How can a settled community have *me* as a member? At times the paradox has seemed to us insoluble, like that of the tourist who travels in search of a haven unvisited by tourists. And at times it has seemed as though we are not settled in this place but flying above it like Icarus, tempting the sun to melt our wings.

There are two types of people in the postmodern economy – those who really do things and the consultants who advise them. Our neighbours are doers through and through, producers of milk, meat, eggs and fodder, without whose honest work all food would be imported, and our landscape left to decay. But for every farmer, builder or shopkeeper there are a thousand consultants, offering themselves as the indispensable mediators between producer and consumer, or between one consultant and another. The City is one vast interlocking consultancy, each person advising the next on questions that exist only because someone is there to advise on them. Westminster is run by consultants: lobbyists, press agents, and spin doctors. Most MPs have started life as consultants, and virtually all the professions have their roots in consultancy.

The evidence is everywhere that if you want to be effective in the new economy, then you must find the niche that enables you to offer advice to people who never previously needed it. The postmodern economy is sometimes described as a 'knowledge economy', although its principal industries (TV for instance) are devoted to the propagation of ignorance. It is more plausible to see the postmodern economy as a fiction – a vast self-perpetuating pretence, in which most people work as hard as they can at doing nothing, and are rewarded with goods obtained at rock-bottom price from the few honest labourers.

Shortly after we were married Michael, our neighbour at Horsell's Farm next door, came round to tell us that he was selling up, since he could no longer make a profit on his beef cattle, and therefore could no longer service his debt. Over dinner we decided to take the plunge. If we bought Mike's farm we could re-brand it as a consultancy. We would follow Muriel Latow's example, and weave our premodern neighbours into a postmodern web. We would redeem their labour, by raising it from the level of fact to that of fiction. This was the task which we set ourselves, and our bank – which consists largely of young consultants – agreed to support us. Thus was founded Horsell's Morsels Ltd, as a path-breaking venture in rural consultancy, offering logic chopping by the metric tonne.

Already we are a fully integrated part of the rural economy. This time four years ago nobody in the Wiltshire claylands needed literary criticism, media relations, musicology or dream-management. Now these are thriving local industries, for the very reason that nobody needs them. Here is an example of our unique enterprise. Three years ago the University of London staged a large international conference on the music of Janáček. At a certain point the organisers approached me, being short of a keynote speech. What was there to be said about Janáček that had not been said a thousand times? For several days wheels were turning at Horsell's Morsels, faxes were flying, internet websites were appearing and disappearing on our busy screens. We discovered 25 studies of Janáček's use of speech-melody and speech-rhythm; several exhaustive biographies; analyses in depth of harmony, rhythm, melody and structure. Every opera pulled to pieces and put back together again 20 times or more. Then that untranslated and untranslateable textbook that he wrote on harmony! Clearly the case was hopeless.

In the oak tree that dominates the hedge in Hanging Hill, an owl has made its nest. It was to this spot one evening that Horsell's Morsels' staff – the Scrutons, three horses, and Stuart the groom – repaired, worn out from their day's researches, and hoping to be refreshed by the view. We watched the sunset paint the sky over Malmesbury Abbey; mist was gathering in the dark seams of the valley, and the newly-cut hedgerows made black crosses on every rise, like memorials to the many dead. The horses stood motionless, pricking their ears at the distant sounds of traffic, their quiet breath lacing the air. A religious silence fell over Horsell's Morsels, and into this silence the owl cried out.

Hearing this eerie call from beyond the grave, with the history of the great Abbey and its religious quest laid out before us on the landscape, I understood what Janáček was expressing in the concluding piece of his piano cycle 'On an Overgrown Path'. The hymn-like tune that constantly starts and breaks off, the owl's cry always interrupting, the inconclusive Tristan chord on which it ends – these things symbolize not death, but the ever-renewing cycle of life. And listening again to the owl's hair-raising call, it seemed to me that the repeated notes in the heart of it, which Janáček writes as a triplet, are in fact four notes, not three. In this way, Horsell's Morsels, by a joint effort involving all the staff, discovered something new to say about Janáček.

Our metafarming has brought new employment to this valley – the first in many years. Our business requires a farm and its manager, horses and groom, an office assistant and part-time workers in all the odd jobs of maintenance and repair. The sobering fact is that none of these people can now be found in our neighbourhood. Although we briefly enjoyed the services of Sidney's daughter, who had just graduated in biology from Oxford and was therefore able to help us with a commission concerning animal welfare, she soon left to become a teacher, hoping to repay her debt to Malmesbury School. The others employed on our farm are either reverse commuters like Roddy, travellers like John, people who work from home in some similar enterprise, or casual 'journeymen' as they used to be called, whose identity we prefer not to know. Moreover, confronted by the real cost of running a farm, in terms of wages, materials, feeds, repairs, machinery, we were struck with renewed admiration for our neighbours, who had hitherto met this cost entirely from farming. With a small amount of farming and a large dose of metafarming we could just about manage; farming alone would have ruined us.

The socialist assault on renting, and the influx of wealthy commuters, have combined to place rural accommodation beyond the reach of the only workers that a farmer could afford to employ. No farmer in his right mind will keep a cottage for a labourer, when the chances are that he could never get rid of him, and when the demise of renting has in any case made it more profitable to sell the cottage. Hence our neighbours struggle to survive on no labour but their own, and are noticeably slowing down under the burden.

Being postmodern farmers, whose labour consists in putting inverted commas around the labour of others, we need a farmhand, groom and manager, and those three functions were until recently performed by a single person. Work-shy school-leavers, girls hooked on ponies and pop, travellers with time on their hands, odd-job men from Swindon – all have been and gone, leaving the place in ever deeper chaos.

Then Terry appeared. He came because Jilly – or was it Hugo? – had sent him as a stand-in. Young, quiet, good-looking, he took immediately to the horses who took immediately to him. He could drive the tractor, trim the hedges, saw the logs, harrow the fields. He could paint, build, ride and muck out. He could handle sheep, clear ditches, plant willows, put up fences. He was willing, energetic and polite. And – best of all – he had a house of his own! We did our sums, cancelled the holiday, sold what Sophie swore to be her very last piece of jewellery (a pair of kitsch earrings I had always disliked), emptied the babies' piggy bank, and made an offer of full-time employment that Terry couldn't – or at any rate didn't – refuse.

That was three years ago, and for a while we were riding high, not least because we no longer did the riding. But then came the blow: Terry's is a postmodern household, the house being the property of his partner. And because partnerships are now provisional, the day must come – and did come very soon – when Terry lacked a home. The choice was stark: find a place for Terry or lose him. All of a sudden we too became part of the rural crisis. Terry's wages could not support a mortgage – not around here; there are no rooms to rent and no tied cottages. In despair we contemplated the final solution – final because it spelled the death of our incomers' innocence: the mobile home behind the hedgerow, the half-concealed transgression against the values and laws that had brought us here in the first place.

And then one day, scanning the world with our new shelter-hungry eyes, we discovered a plain brick box, with Edwardian sash windows, standing in a paddock by the road. We had often passed it, but had always overlooked it, as you overlook an old hut by the railway or a trailer in a field. It was divided down the middle, to form two semi-detached houses, one of which was empty, the other done up with potted plants. We learned that the house belonged to the Nolans who farm at the end of our road; the potted plants hid Granny; the other half was empty. Unheated, unfurnished, this damp, thin structure looks from its large windows across the fields in our direction: the perfect observation post, with the kind of bracing atmosphere and raw invincible chill that could only serve to attach Terry more deeply to the bleak, wet, wuthering life of Sundey Hill.

Another holiday cancelled, the very last piece of jewellery again confessed to (an art deco bracelet set with opals, actually rather appealing), the piggy bank re-raided, and we finally put together a plausible rent. But the Nolans hesitate. 'Now if Terry were prepared to put in a few hours here and there, especially at hay-making...'. Hoping to create a new tie, we discover, we have merely revived the old one. Terry continued working for us; but for the first time in years the Nolans had their own farm labourer in their own tied cottage. And as so often, this return to the old world had been subsidized by people who came from the new.

Cobbett, in his well-meant endeavours to stop the farm labourers of his day from smashing the machines that were casting them out of work, insisted that farmers were no different from other industrial workers, whose best interest was ultimately served by adopting the most efficient way to produce their goods. 'For indeed, what is a farmer other than a manufacturer of corn and cattle?', he wrote.[33]

The answer is obvious. The farmer is not a manufacturer at all. He is esteemed for his product. But he is esteemed far more for his by-product. Our somewhere was shaped by human hands; it bears the mark of a culture, a moral inheritance and a store of practical knowledge. It is not nature but nature imprinted with a human face – for such is any genuine landscape. The English countryside is not being destroyed by farm subsidies, for these maintain the people who maintain it. Far more damaging are the hidden subsidies offered to the motor industry, to business parks and to the supermarkets. Yet even the supermarkets could be integrated into our microsphere if they learned the art of buying local produce and retailing it through village stores, so returning their subsidies to the people who ultimately fund them.

One of our more pleasurable commissions has been to advise a supermarket chain on how to re-brand itself as a local store, selling local produce to local people, in ways that reaffirm the relations between neighbours. The project awoke us to the narrowness of the gap – a gap created almost entirely by needless regulations – between our neighbours and the people who would like to buy from them. Consider milk: the commodity to which our community has been devoted, and through which it most keenly feels the pinch of unfair competition, uncompensated regulation, and hidden subsidies. The cow is the most efficient device ever discovered for turning grass into human food. Without cows, our stretch of country would never have acquired its human population. It would be unthinkable that a French farmer, faced with the collapse of milk prices, should not turn to cheese-making, or that he should be deterred by the EU regulations which ostensibly aim to stamp out this cottage industry but which are really designed, in the French view of things, to foster a healthy habit of disobedience.

In Virgil's *Georgics*, which tell of expropriations and famine, cheese is a symbol of hospitality, the thing that can be stored in times of abundance and brought forth in times of want. It is the proof of self-sufficiency and of the peasant's title to his home. Cheese still has this function in the Mediterranean, and a whole cheese placed before a guest remains an incomparable form of welcome – a way of saying that I, the host, am settled here, and you, the wanderer, can share my wise provisions. Thanks to the supermarket chains, our cheese has lost this hospitable significance: it is an industrial product, sold in sterilized slabs, and its generic names – Cheddar, Cheshire, Lancashire – retain no trace of their geographical meaning or of the old arts of the dairy. Cheese has changed from thing to stuff: in English the word has all but lost its plural, and the principal sign that a cheese has been made, not manufactured – the rind that shuts it in and forms its boundary – has been banished from the market.

Yet the British Cheese Awards that take place each autumn in Stow-on-the-Wold and which are ignored by the Government and by DEFRA give heart-warming proof that the British people can apply their enterprising instincts as well to cheese-making (the traditional occupation of the claylands until the last war) as to the manufacture of widgets. Over 700 cheeses were entered to be judged in 2001, compared with less than 300 in 1994 when the awards began. Many of them were the produce of small farms and individual enthusiasts, and the best were as good as anything available in Italy or France. These new British cheeses laid claim to an individual existence: circles, globes, pyramids, cones and hexagons, each tightly bound by rind, beckoning to be taken away and stored entire for the winter. Not stuff but things – substances in Aristotle's, rather than Bacon's, sense. The unpasteurized 'Celtic Promise' that I acquired for my family was a flattened ball, with a speckled brownish rind protecting a soft, rich interior, like a soft-boiled yolk: a distillation of grass into protein which had the beauty and perfection of an egg. Moreover, to my astonishment the cheese that won first prize in 2001 was made near here, by Marion Conisbee-Smith of North Cerney, who produced a raw-milk cheese imbued with those farmyard flavours that pasteurization boils away. Needless to say, the bureaucrats are trying their hardest to kill off the use of raw milk in cheese; but that is just one more reason to hope that the renewed enthusiasm for cheese-making will penetrate down to the dairy farmer, and so make this product available – as real meat and real milk are still available – in the black economy.

Many of those who wrote about the farming crisis at the end of the nineteenth century blamed the squirearchy for the collapse of village life. J. Arthur Gibbs, for example, writing in 1903 of villages not far from here, argued that the local squires owed their unpopularity to their invisibility, shutting themselves away at weekends with their house guests, while earning and spending in London.[34] The squire is now a thing of the past; but the incomer has replaced him, earning and spending everywhere but the place where he lives.

This lack of connection between the incomers and the people who maintain the view from their windows is noticeable in the changed politics of our district. Once a county of safe Conservative seats, Wiltshire is now closely fought between Conservatives and Liberal Democrats in the rural parts, and between both parties and Labour in the towns. The demographic reality behind this change was brought home to me at the last election, when I set out to canvas our village in the Conservative interest.

If you have ever wondered why politicians have such a tough, leathery exterior and such an irresolute emptiness inside, then you should go canvassing. The effect of this close encounter with the British people in circumstances calculated to elicit an opinion is profoundly traumatic. To do it all the time, as politicians must, exposing yourself to harangues, stares, rumours of conspiracy and sudden manic laughs is like having repeated transfusions of the wrong type of blood. And should someone make threatening gestures or throw a rotten tomato, your first inclination is to think that you have somehow deserved it, that this direct glimpse into the opinionated darkness of the democratic mind is beyond the pale of British manners.

There is a council estate in our village, a red-tiled, concrete-panelled eyesore from the 50s, well seeded at the time with Labour stalwarts. We have no Labour candidate, however, and Labour supporters have only one opportunity to vent their political passions, which is when opening the door to a canvasser. Most of them are Old Labour by persuasion and most of them are old in any case: trade unionists, road menders, railway workers, incomers to the old rural economy who have no place in the new.

They come to the door angry and trembling in their collarless shirts, to tell you that they are not the least bit interested in anything you have to say, that this country has gone downhill ever since that woman was put in charge of it, that the new lot are no better, and in any case here are the 100 things that need to be put right before anyone has *my* vote. Sometimes I attempt to impart my own political philosophy. Voting, I say, is a choice among evils; one is a Tory only *on balance*, so to speak. The best we can hope for is to be governed, as it were, in a spirit of compromise. It all sounds very fair-minded and democratic.

The only good result of this speech is that it causes the monologue to give way to a hostile and uncomprehending stare. As I make my escape I look with longing at the green fields beyond the council estate, where the farmers have already put their blue placards in the hedgerows, and where I shall go to enjoy a more soothing flood of mindless prejudice just as soon as the last concrete house has been canvassed.

In fact this last house is my most pleasant port of call. The door opens and four happy children fall out, bouncing down the steps like rubber skittles, and landing in a heap on the pavement. They stay there, propping each other up in doll-like poses, each producing one section of a broad collective smile. Mother and father are young, handsome, and they too are smiling. The house has an air of easy-going routine: raincoats hang in the hallway, shoes beneath, and a hat-stand laden with garden-tools sways as the father steps past. On the whitewashed wall is a print of Monet's water lilies, and beyond the far door a clean and tidy kitchen shines in a spasm of sun. For the first time that morning I catch sight of a book, turned upside down on the kitchen table. The couple are undecided voters, they tell me, but as soon as there's a moment, they'll sit down and think about it. Meanwhile they are grateful for the leaflets, happy to converse about the state of the world and the weather, and in general delighted to postpone a choice that might make them differ from their neighbours. All in all, a wonderful advertisement for the undecided mind.

The council estate was built for a previous generation of incomers – those who manned the railway station that Lord Beeching took away from our village, and who lived by union rules. The present generation of incomers comes to us by quite another route. Every now and then one of the farmers appeals to his Tory friends on the council for permission to build the little close of houses that will rescue him from bankruptcy, and every now and then permission is granted. These little islands of suburbia with their two-car garages and gravel drives are filled with Liberal Democrats, who lecture me in their Scottish accents about the need to modernize our country, and about the damage done by 1000 years of Tory misrule. No chance of using my spiel about the lesser evil: theirs is a worldview in which evil is absolute, and I myself the proof of it.

My round ends at a small farm by the crossroads, where two brothers – known, I am later told, as Nim-Nim and Pardon – live with their herd of cows. Nim-Nim, a thin man of about 50, has a dull, reliable look like John Major, and his jaw wobbles as he drenches me with speech. Like John Major, he sounds very serious and well-informed; however he has improved on the archetype's vocabulary, boiling it down to the single syllable 'nim'. His older brother appears, a large, strapping man who responds to my overtures by cupping one hand to an ear and shouting 'Pardon?'. Nim-Nim translates what I have said into strings of monosyllables and at last understanding dawns. The brothers look at each other for a moment, and then, in a wobbling unison, Pardon shouting and Nim-Nim mouthing, declare 'We don't vote'. They give me a disarming look, implying that they had formed this policy a long time ago, on the strength of a general theory about the rights of imbeciles. And I go away with the thought of how nice it would be if others followed their example.

Nim-Nim and Pardon are vivid testimony to the fate of rural society. Young people with energy and ambition leave, and those who remain are not conscious of having espoused a lost cause only because they are frequently not conscious of anything. But if old photographs are anything to go by, this development is by no means a recent one.

Nowadays no one sits for a photograph without smiling into the camera – no one, that is, save fashion models, who adopt a frozen and narcissitic scowl. Even politicians, clergymen and artists have adopted this habit of smiling into the void, attempting to have with everyone a relationship that can be had only with someone. In old farms you encounter photographs of the old kind, showing people still endeavouring to vindicate their lives to the curious stranger. Houses which stay in the same hands for generations become frames, whose occupants stand in them as though posed for a portrait. On the mantelpiece or in the hall you find generations of these sober unsmiling people, each striving to fill the space allotted him before relinquishing it to his heirs.

When Crispin's father acquired the old farm down the road, he discovered a large sepia-toned photograph of the couple who had lived there a century ago. They are sitting on sturdy mahogany chairs in front of their panelled door, she in a full-length cotton dress with pleated sleeves and he in a woollen suit and waistcoat, the buttons of which strain against the cloth. Both have hats – hers a flower-strewn dome above its frisbee rim, his a banded trilby. And both hold their large hands folded in their laps as they stare beyond the camera at their unknown judges. They belong to no particular moment, and show no particular emotion. Their eyes are still and their thin lips firmly set against speech. They have composed themselves into the picture and not themselves only – their farm, their ownership, their work and their way of life, entwined around them like an ancient briar.

As you study them, however, a curious fact begins to dawn on you. They have the same bulbous nose, the same narrow eyes behind identical spectacles, the same thin lips and pendant ears, the same wedge-shaped furrows along the cheeks, the same potato-shaped heads, the same posture, hands, shoulders and widespread hips. In short, they are identical – if not twins, then certainly brother and sister. In their effort to wipe away their private world, to stand proud and right and true in the eyes of judgement, they have exposed precisely what they no doubt strove to conceal from day to day, as she hid in the kitchen and he bent his weathered form behind the plough. This most respectable couple, emulating the dignities of the yeoman farmer, were in fact a pair of incestuous hideaways.

And then there are the two photographs on the stairs of Crispin's farm, touched up into crude simulacra of oil paintings. These show hydrocephalic children in their Sunday suits, both staring from wild disconnected eyes to each side of the camera. Is this not an equal revelation of a hidden truth, a proof that these people were not, as the portraits pretend, breeding and thriving, but expiring like the Neanderthal as the new world encroached?

Study such photographs and you will surely conclude that, if farming has survived, it is because people from outside the community have saved the gene-pool from stagnation. Although Sidney's farm has been in his family for 200 years, and although his name is recorded on ancient tombstones in Somerford church, he, like his father before him, has married an incomer. His daughter Anna, who joined our consultancy, and who learned through us the arts of typesetting, editing and speaking to the press, is an Oxford graduate. Another is still at university, but takes charge of the milking during vacations; a third is doing brilliantly at school. Sidney's wife is a graduate in English, writes in her spare time, and is active on committees both locally and in London. Sidney belongs to every little platoon in our district, from the skittles club to the hunt, and from the parents' association to the farmers' supper club. He has diversified from dairy farming into horse breeding and veal, and from time to time contributes his wry and deeply felt observations to *The Countryman*, a magazine founded in 1927 as the voice of the first generation of urban incomers, and which has iconized the English countryside as the goal of our wanderings and the source of our strength.[35]

No-one has extended a greater welcome to us than Sidney, for whom we represent a new kind of support, not merely for farming, but for the kind of rural life that he wants his daughters to enjoy. It is by winding our lives together with Sidney's – we employing his daughters, he supplying our milk, we campaigning for his livelihood, he educating us in the ways of the claylands – that we have acquired the knowledge and the skills required to confront our boopoles. At a certain point Horsell's Morsels was commissioned by the *Financial Times* to produce articles about the countryside, and soon the rumour spread that the Scrutons were not merely settling in these parts but also observing the inhabitants. Our neighbours responded by observing us in turn. Our clumsy attempts at farming, which had at first elicited contempt, now became an object of study and a source of pride, conclusive demonstration that real farmers have skills that cannot be easily acquired and which might be a fitting subject for an article. Sidney began to write down his thoughts on farming and to leave them on our doorstep with the milk. And of course it helps to have children. Thresholds that we could never cross dissolve before our children's footsteps, and in Wootton Bassett high street Sam and Lucy receive greetings from people to whom we can barely attach a name.

The neighbours assembled in our house this Christmas, as they have done since Sam was born, for an evening of carols. At a certain point Sidney, who had put on a black tie, interrupted the singing to tell us that he and his daughter Anna had devised a spectacular morality for our instruction. A Punch-and-Judy theatre was brought in, and Anna installed beneath the stage. We were to witness a puppet play accompanied by Sidney's rhyming couplets. A professor from London, with prominent specs and an expression of theatrical naivety, appears on the stage. His life in that remote, dim city is recounted in tones of awe and amazement. One by one his strange writings are lifted from a black magician's case and replaced with a shudder of revulsion – until finally *On Hunting* emerges from the darkness, and the story changes gear. We see the weird professor aboard a train – a steam-train, complete with plumes of smoke, bearing the insignia of the GWR, the kind of train that used to stop at the station next to Sidney's farm. We see the professor astride his horse George, falling, getting up again, falling. We see the dreary courtyards of a London college and the appalled expressions of the professor's colleagues, as the rumours of his new recreation reach their ears. And then we see Sunday Hill Farm, unchanged from the bleak, functional box with metal-framed windows and pig-sties, Sunday Hill Farm as it will forever be in the memories and imaginings of our farming neighbours – a place for sheep and pigs, destined, unless rescued by a miracle, to failure. We see the new horse Barney, and Sophie in her Beaufort uniform, rescuing the hopeless prof from yet another tumble. And the story moves towards its happy ending, with undisguised endorsement of the couple whose decision to settle in the claylands is the goal and the moral of it all.

Puppets can be true to life as no actor can be, since the life that we imagine in them is ours. Sidney's puppet play was greeted with shouts of acclamation by our neighbours, because it prompted them not to see us but to imagine us, and to imagine us as belonging at last with them. The children were puzzled by what they had seen – why, in particular, hadn't Punch bashed Judy? But the company returned with renewed enthusiasm to their carols.

Concerning Christmas I am of the Scrooge school of thought, being as distressed by the plastic rubbish that the children are given as by the acquisitive gestures with which they claw it from its packaging. Nevertheless, in recent years my attitude has softened. In our place faith in the Christ-child is a shy but public acknowledgement of a spiritual bequest. Each school ends the term with a nativity play, and you can witness your child in the costume of shepherd, star or angel, framed in his 'angel infancy'. For our neighbours Christmas is a time of giving, rather than a time of getting and spending. And among the gifts offered to the incomer is the supreme gift of acceptance.

The carol singing over, and the guests departed, we sit for a while in front of our wood burner to meditate on what the Christian faith still means. 'Emmanuel' – God with us, sharing our mortality and accepting death at our hands – is at once so strange and so consoling an idea that we prefer to hide it in stories and to protect it from rational disproof. The Christmas story is one of peace and goodwill, brought to us by the lamb that we ourselves will sacrifice. It outlines the unifying myth of our rural culture and the spiritual meaning of our English ways of settlement. Yet there is, growing in our midst, a violent antipathy not merely to that mystical idea, but also to the civilization that speaks through it, and which has made a tolerant scepticism one part of its moral outlook.

According to the Koran, the fire in which we infidels shall burn is never-ending, and its victims never consumed. Our hides will be renewed from time to time in order to refresh our torments. Such, apparently, is the decree of Allah, the compassionate, the merciful. I humbly submit that someone has made a mistake here, concerning either the punishment or its author. Although the members of al-Qa'eda would be happy for us to put the matter to the test, we prefer to sit for a few more years beside our fire at home, postponing the time of judgement and watching the logs as they settle in the flames. For if God intended there to be a fire that burns unendingly, it is surely this one, that warms the body and brings peace to the soul. Embossed in old Norwegian dialect on the cast-iron Jøtul stove in our sitting room – Sam's pretend television and the source of all our warmth – are the following words:

> *I rake down my fire late in the evening when the day is done.*
> *God grant that my fire may never go out.*

We do our best to live up to this inscription. Retiring, we rake the embers, add a log or two and close the vent. The stove then burns all night, so that the house needs no other heating.

The enamel fires in my parents' suburban house were fuelled with coke and coal; to light them was the work of half an hour, and they burned with a lifeless glow amid a blue aurora of poison. As soon as they could afford it my parents switched to gas and then to oil-fired central heating: in other words from one fossil fuel to another. The fire with which bin Laden threatens us is also fuelled by fossils – by the fossilized forests beneath the sands of Arabia, and the fossilized religion in the air above. Fossils are the greatest threat to our planet, and I don't doubt that there is an old Norwegian proverb that says: what God has buried, don't dig up.

Those who burn logs burn renewable energy; and in growing their fuel they extract from the atmosphere all the carbon that their fires release. In yet another sense, therefore, their fires burn unendingly, and if the sustainable is our modern equivalent of the eternal, we wood-burners must be counted among the saved. Our old hedgerows contain ash, hawthorn and crab-apple, along with the usual dead elms and blackthorn. All logs burn well in our Jøtul television, and when the door is thrown open, whatever the fuel, you see a fairy landscape where flames dance over shifting cinders and sparks flock together like migrating birds, before circling away in the chimney.

Willingly I join the generations who have dreamed at the hearth, and found in the changing landscape of a murmuring fire some presentiment of human destiny. In the apocalypse market, I much prefer the Scandinavian to the Arabian product. With that uncanny insight which caused Claude Lévi-Strauss to praise him as the founder of structuralist anthropology, Wagner saw that the old myth of Wotan-Odin concealed the sacred ritual of a vegetation cult. Wotan must die as trees die, to be reborn in some future spring. It is the world ash-tree – the tree of Wotan's spear – that is hewn in logs for the final conflagration, and ash, we have discovered, burns with the greatest flame. Many are the interpretations to which *The Ring of the Nibelung* lends itself. But one thing that it seems to say is that God, like the ash tree, is a renewable resource, and lives and dies eternally.

And what of the soil? Is that too a renewable resource? Our somewhere lies on the edge of nowhere, like the little patch of earth in Brueghel's picture. And like Brueghel's ploughman our people ignore the noise and commotion that are unsettling the wider world. They direct their eyes to solitary tasks, and their skills to turning earth to profit, muck to brass. They have taught us the value of many things: of patience and sacrifice, of rooted loves and settled customs. Observing them we have learned that the soil is indeed a renewable resource. But it is renewed by the virtues of those who live in it, and not by edicts from elsewhere.

Notes

1. Sundey Hill, but Sunday Hill Farm, Sundays Hill Farm (our next door neighbour), Sundeys Hill Farm, Upper Sundey Hill Farm, and so on, in the effort to distinguish barns and cottages that once were nameless.
2. James Howard Kunstler, *The Geography of Nowhere: the Rise and Decline of America's Man-made Landscape*, New York, 1993.
3. *Metamorphoses*, VIII, 217–20.
4. W. H. Auden, 'Musée des Beaux-Arts'. Auden's vision of the painting is reiterated, for example, by W. G. Sebald, that unsettled observer of the English way of settling, in *After Nature*, tr. Michael Hamburger, London, 2002, p. 104.
5. John Aubrey, *Natural History of Wiltshire*, 1685, ed. John Britton, London, 1847, p. 11.
6. Arthur Young (1741–1820), the most dedicated of all our writers on agriculture, was secretary to the newly created Board of Agriculture (1793), and editor of the monthly *Annals of Agriculture* (1784–1809), whose contributors included Jeremy Bentham, King George III (writing as Ralph Robinson), Coke of Holkham and many others who saw the transformation in agriculture as the crucial issue of their time.
7. Evan Eisenberg, *Back to Eden*.
8. H. Rider Haggard, *A Farmer's Year, being his commonplace book for 1898*, London, 1899, p. 14.
9. See Graham Harvey, *The Forgiveness of Nature: The Story of Grass*, London, 2001.
10. Fanny Kingsley, *Life and Works of Charles Kingsley*, Vol. 1, London, 1901.
11. Alfred Schutz, 'Making Music Together', in *Collected Papers*, 2 vols., The Hague, 1964.
12. See the illuminating discussion of cremation in Ken Worpole, *Last Landscapes*, London, 2003, pp. 162–3.
13. See 'The Bells', by Walter De La Mare, who disapproved of Pound as Pound did of him.

175

14. The seminal role of the yeoman farmer in shaping the countryside, the laws and the institutions of England has been a leading theme of English historiography, since Macaulay first announced it in his *History of England* (London, 1849–1855). See Alan Macfarlane, *The Origins of English Individualism: the Family, Property and Social Transition*, Oxford, 1986.
15. It is, of course, the male bird that so rapturously sings; but Jenny Wren is an honorary female, like Puss the hare. Other languages lean the other way: in German the wren is *Der Zaunkönig* – king of the fence.
16. Gilbert White, *The Natural History of Selbourne*, Letter XVI, London, 1936.
17. Izaak Walton, *The Compleat Angler* (2nd edition), London, 1655.
18. The bond between falconer and falcon is even harder to form, and yet more deeply settled in the soul, than the bond between ferreter and ferret. See T. H. White, *The Goshawk*, London, 1951.
19. Though festivals at sheep-shearing are of ancient origin, possibly derived from the Roman Parilia.
20. Stephen Budiansky, *The Nature of Horses*, London, 1997.
21. The relevant research is summarized in Mihaly Csikszentmihaly and Robert Kubey, 'Television addiction is no metaphor', *Scientific American*, 23 February 2002.
22. Raymond Briggs, *Ethel and Ernest*, London, 1998: a moving evocation in cartoon-strip images of the culture in which I grew up.
23. Sam and Sam Clark, *Moro – the Cookbook,* London, 2001.
24. *Josser: the Secret Life of a Circus Girl*, by Nell Stroud, London, 2000.
25. Heidegger, not otherwise given to lucid utterance, captures the point well in his essay 'Building and Dwelling'.
26. See the eloquent pleading for the plotlands by Colin Ward and associates (e.g., Dennis Hardy and Colin Ward: *Arcadia for All: the Legacy of a Makeshift Landscape*, London, 1984), for the 'unofficial countryside' by the naturalist Richard Mabey (*The Unofficial Countryside*, London, 1973), and for low-impact development on the edge of things by the estimable Simon Fairlie of Tinker's Bubble, whose *Chapter 7 Newsletter* is available from The Potato Store, Flaxdrayton Farm, South Petherton, Somerset TA13.
27. See Oliver Rackham, *The History of the Countryside*, London, 1986, pp.194 *et seq.*
28. See Friedrich Schneider and Dominik Enste, 'Shadow Economies: Size, Causes and Consequences', *Journal of Economic Literature*, 2000, 38/1, pp.77–114.
29. *Change in the Village*, London, 1912.
30. Raymond Williams, *Culture and Society, 1780–1950*, London, 1958.

31. This is something that Williams himself recognizes in a subsequent work, *The Country and the City*, London, 1973, ch. 4.
32. To go back no further than the agricultural crisis of the late nineteenth century, readers will find 'Agricola' (Sir C. Fielding) anticipating all that is said today in his prophecy (accurate as it turned out) entitled *How England was Saved*, London, 1908, which pointed to the absolute need for an autarkic food economy. As the twentieth century progressed the message of doom did not disappear. But what was originally seen as a national crisis was increasingly described as a global one. See Ann Berkelbach and D.G. Hutton, *The Pinch of Plenty: the World Agrarian Crisis*, London, 1932. For a recent American attack on the subsidy machine, see James Bovard, *The Farm Fiasco*, San Francisco, 1991.
33. William Cobbett, *Political Register*, November 1816.
34. J. Arthur Gibbs, *A Cotswold Village*, London, 1903.
35. Earning thereby the opprobrium of Raymond Williams, who sees the magazine as the voice of the middle-class observer, and therefore an act of treason against the rural labourer and his class (*The Country and the City*, p. 313). But what class is that, I wonder?